God, Creation, and Climate Change

God, Creation, and Climate Change

A Catholic Response to the Environmental Crisis

Richard W. Miller, editor

ORBIS BOOKS

Maryknoll, New York 10545

Founded in 1970, Orbis Books endeavors to publish works that enlighten the mind, nourish the spirit, and challenge the conscience. The publishing arm of the Maryknoll Fathers and Brothers, Orbis seeks to explore the global dimensions of the Christian faith and mission, to invite dialogue with diverse cultures and religious traditions, and to serve the cause of reconciliation and peace. The books published reflect the views of their authors and do not represent the official position of the Maryknoll Society. To learn more about Maryknoll and Orbis Books, please visit our website at www.maryknollsociety.org.

Copyright © 2010 by Richard W. Miller.

Published by Orbis Books, Maryknoll, New York 10545-0302.

Manufactured in the United States of America.

Library of Congress Cataloging-in-Publication Data

God, creation, and climate change : a Catholic response to the
    environmental crisis / edited by Richard W. Miller.
        p. cm.
    ISBN 978-1-57075-889-8 (pbk.)
    1. Human ecology – Religious aspects – Catholic Church.
  2. Environmentalism – Religious aspects – Catholic Church.
  3. Catholic Church – Doctrines. I. Miller, Richard W., II.
BX1795.H82G64 2010
261.8′8 – dc22   2010004049

Contents

Introduction

Richard W. Miller

Since the publication of the Intergovernmental Panel on Climate Change (IPCC) Fourth Assessment Report in 2007 more and more scientists have been speaking out about the dire consequences of inaction with respect to climate change and environmental degradation. The hierarchy in the Roman Catholic communion has been addressing this issue for many years, as the scientific assessment of our present situation has made it painfully clear that our present path is unsustainable and has destructive consequences for large parts of both nonhuman creation and human beings. Pope Benedict XVI has addressed this issue consistently and quite forcefully, most especially in his encyclical *Charity in Truth* and his recent Message for the World Day of Peace "If You Want to Cultivate Peace, Protect Creation."

The magnitude of the problem of environmental degradation in general and climate change in particular requires a complete rethinking and reorienting of our way of being in the world. Responding to the present environmental crisis requires not only a conversion of the will but even more fundamentally a transformation of the imagination.[1] The imagination is the capacity to think of other possible ways of being, thinking, and acting in the world. The essays in this volume contribute to such a transformation of our imaginations.

The first essay, "Global Climate Disruption and Social Justice: The State of the Problem," is intended to aid the reader in imagining the possibilities for the planet and the human community, especially the poor, that the scientific community warns us of, as well as the possibilities open to humanity to change its present course. I make it clear that this is one of the greatest social justice issues in human history; yet the American public is largely unaware of the magnitude of the problem, the enormous potential of renewable energies to meet current and future energy needs, and the great human resources in the United States to effect change.

It is widely recognized that at the root of the modern dominance of the natural world — which is leading to widespread destruction of the foundations of human existence and the existence of a great number of species and ecosystems — is a type of thinking in which human beings understand themselves as the center of the created world (i.e., anthropocentrism). Some critics maintain that the Judeo-Christian tradition strongly validates and supports this anthropocentric viewpoint in its understanding of the human being as the apex and goal of creation. Professor Dianne Bergant, C.S.A., in the second essay, "The Bible's Wisdom Tradition and Creation Theology" explores the supposed anthropocentrism in the scriptures through an examination of the account of creation in the wisdom tradition of Israel, in particular through a reading of the book of Job and the Wisdom of Solomon. This reading shows the crucial significance of creation theology to all of theology.

While the second essay criticizes anthropocentric readings of central texts of the Old Testament and then draws upon these texts to aid in rethinking and reimagining the place of human beings in the larger created world, the third and fourth essays invite us to rethink and reimagine central Christian doctrines in the tradition in light of the present environmental crisis. The third essay, "Creation, Incarnation, and Resurrection," reflects upon central Christian doctrines, especially the doctrine of the resurrection, to criticize the tendency by some important figures in the tradition to spiritualize the resurrection. Spiritualizing the resurrection leads to a diminished view of human beings' materiality and an undervaluing of the nonhuman creation. This spiritualization of the resurrection was a result of the influence of Neo-Platonism on Christianity. John O'Keefe proposes that a recovery of Irenaeus of Lyon's pre-Platonic vision of the resurrection is the best way to correct the negative aspects of the Platonic tradition and will lead to a greater sense of the value of human materiality and the nonhuman creation.

The fourth essay, "Environmental Degradation, Social Sin, and the Common Good," continues the movement in theology, seen especially in liberation theology in Latin America, to broaden the notion of personal sin, as a particular human being's offense against God, to social sin, as institutionalized patterns of human behavior and actions that are antithetical to the reign of God because they are destructive and degrading of the full humanity of human beings.

Professor Jame Schaefer argues that a host of ecological problems, including human-forced changes to the global climate, requires an even more comprehensive concept, "planetary sin." Planetary sin includes both personal sin and social sin; yet it extends these notions to the nonhuman creation, the species and ecosystems that are necessary for the sustainability of the planet. The poor and vulnerable among us now include the poor and vulnerable species and ecosystems that are susceptible to human domination. As Schaefer extends the notions of sin and the poor and vulnerable beyond human beings to include other species and natural systems, she also extends the notion of the common good to include the planetary common good. The planetary common good (i.e., the internal sustainability and flourishing of the earth) must be pursued, a pursuit empowered by God's grace, through solidarity with all species and biological systems of which human beings are an integral part. Such solidarity requires a system of ethics that demands action at all levels of society to assure a life-sustaining planet.

While the fourth essay treats the problem of institutional, systemic, or social sin, the fifth essay, "Theology and Sustainable Economics," examines perhaps the central system in modern life that is driving ecological degradation, namely, the economy. Professor Daniel Finn argues that there are four fundamental problems that every economy needs to resolve: the allocation of productive resources to produce goods and services, the distribution of what is produced to people in the society, the scale of human economic activity within finite limits, and the quality of economic relationships. Markets provide an effective, though not perfect, resolution of the first problem of allocating productive resources to produce goods and services. Markets, however, offer dramatically inadequate answers to the other three problems of distribution of what is produced, the scale of human economic activity, and the quality of economic relationships. Finn argues that Christian theology, especially its understanding of the place of the material world in God's creation, can offer principles to guide both personal decisions and public policy. He correlates the insights of theology and economics to help move toward a just and sustainable future.

After thinking through the magnitude of the environmental problem, especially with regards to climate change, and then retrieving the scriptural, doctrinal, and social teachings of the Catholic community to reimagine and rethink the relationship of human beings to the nonhuman creation, the final essay responds to the question: What is to be done? David O'Brien in his essay, "Another Call to Action: Catholics and the Challenge of Climate Change," reflects upon the Catholic community's participation in social movements, past and present, to assist the present response to the environmental crisis. He reconsiders the importance of shared civic responsibility in contemporary American life and how the churches can best encourage support for the common good in the face of such an immense issue.

These essays originated as talks at the Seventh Annual Church in the 21st Century Lecture Series held in Kansas City, Missouri, on September 26, 2009.[2] Many of the papers have been updated since they were originally presented. The final chapter of this book, however, has not been updated. It is a transcript of the lively panel discussion from the conference. This panel discussion initiates a conversation that should begin advancing through parishes and other Catholic institutions across the United States because as the pope's message for the 2010 World Day of Peace makes clear, if it is peace and justice that we seek, we must protect creation.

Notes

1. This line of thinking is influenced by Paul Ricoeur's statement: "Is it not because we too often and too quickly think of a will that submits and not enough of an imagination that opens itself?" Paul Ricoeur, "Toward a Hermeneutic of the Idea of Revelation," in Paul Ricoeur, *Essays on Biblical Interpretation,* ed. Lewis S. Mudge (Philadelphia: Fortress Press, 1980), 73–118 at 117.

2. The other books that have come out of this lecture series are: *Women through the Ages: Women and the Shaping of Catholicism,* ed. Richard W. Miller (Liguori, Mo.: Liguori Press, 2009); *We Hold These Truths: Catholicism and American Political Life,* ed. Richard W. Miller (Liguori, Mo.: Liguori Press, 2008); *Prayer in the Catholic Tradition,* ed. Richard W. Miller II (Liguori, Mo.: Liguori Press, 2007); *Spirituality for the 21st Century: Experiencing God in the Catholic Tradition,* ed. Richard W. Miller II (Liguori, Mo.: Liguori Press, 2006); *Lay Ministry in the Catholic Church: Visioning Church Ministry through the Wisdom of the Past,* ed. Richard W. Miller II (Liguori, Mo.: Liguori Press, 2005); *The Catholic Church in the 21st Century: Finding Hope for Its Future in the Wisdom of Its Past,* ed. Rev. Michael J. Himes (Liguori, Mo.: Liguori Press, 2004).

ONE

Global Climate Disruption and Social Justice

THE STATE OF THE PROBLEM

Richard W. Miller

THERE ARE A HOST of examples of environmental degradation that endanger species and stress ecosystems throughout the world. In this essay, I will focus on the problem of global warming and greenhouse gas pollution because climate change is going to affect everything; it is the whole that will affect all the parts. Furthermore, I shall focus primarily on how climate change will impact human beings. The polar bear has in many ways become the face of climate change. When the media focuses its cameras on demonstrators at international climate meetings they inevitably focus the cameras on young protesters wearing polar bear masks. The young protesters behind those masks will be as much the victims of climate change as the polar bear. While my focus is to get us to think of the human cost of climate change, I am cognizant that there are very real and important questions about our responsibilities as Christians for the preservation of species. Some have argued that we are in this terrible predicament primarily because of anthropocentric thinking that is blind to the true value of the nonhuman creation. This larger issue will be touched upon in later essays. For now, however, I want to focus on the way human beings could be impacted by climate change.

The Dangerous Gap between Scientific Knowledge and Public Awareness

James Hansen of NASA's Goddard Space Center is arguably the most distinguished climate scientist in the world. Hansen maintains,

1

"A wide gap has developed between what is understood about global warming by the relevant scientific community and what is known by policymakers and the public."[1] Hansen's comment is supported by data. According to a recent article in *Eos,* which is a journal of the American Geophysical Union, 97 percent of specialists surveyed think that human activity is a significant contributing factor in changing the mean global temperature compared to 58 percent of the general public.[2] There are many reasons for this disparity; I will focus on four central reasons. First, global warming does not always coincide with our immediate experience. This summer in the Midwest, for instance, was the coolest summer that I can remember. Some people think this means that global warming is not happening. A single cool summer or especially cold winter does not refute the truth that the climate is warming. Global climate is the average weather over a long period of time for the whole globe. While there can be variations year to year, the average of the weather over time and space indicates that the globe is warming. Furthermore, while I experienced this summer as unusually cool, the Midwestern part of the United States represents a minuscule portion of the total surface area of the globe. Indeed, the contiguous forty-eight states of the United States represent only 1.5 percent of the total surface area of the globe.[3] The National Oceanic and Atmospheric Association's National Climatic Data Center has reported that "the combined global land and ocean average surface temperature for June–August 2009 was the third warmest on record for the season."[4] While temperatures in the Midwest were cooler than average, temperatures near the Arctic were as high as 9 degrees Fahrenheit (5 degrees Celsius) above average.[5]

While I might not feel the effects of global warming in my daily life, this does not mean that it is not going on. The very fact that many of us do not really experience or feel the effects of global warming is an enormous problem. It provides the conditions for us to be deceived by misinformation campaigns by oil companies and coal companies and leads to either a denial of global warming or a complacency concerning it. We have a highly limited, uninformed perspective in our everyday life so that we have no sense of the vital signs of the planet. Let me give an example to illustrate this point. In 1994, I visited a good family friend in the hospital. When I visited him he looked good, he was chatting away, he looked and acted like he always had. He appeared to be physically fit and in good spirits. In looking at him I could not recognize any problem. The doctors, who had been running tests on him, said that he had a rare form of leukemia that spreads very rapidly and that he was going to be fighting for his life. The only outward sign that there was a problem was a deep purple mark on his forearm. Without the doctors' expertise, I would have thought that it was a bruise. I would have had no idea that he was fighting for his life. Indeed, he did not recognize that anything was wrong until this mark emerged on his arm and another sore appeared on his tongue. The doctors and medical specialists, however, were trained so that they could do tests to determine the state of his health. While I saw nothing, the tests performed by the doctors revealed the magnitude of the problem. Sadly, they were right. In three weeks, he was dead at the age of fifty-two. Where we are in terms of global warming is a little bit like this. Everything seems fairly normal for us in the Midwest, and for much of the United States the signs of global warming are not apparent in people's daily lives, but thousands of specialists who are trained in reading the vital signs of the planet are exclaiming that we are in a planetary emergency.

This medical example is also illustrative of our belief in science. When my friend had this unexplained mark on his arm, he saw a doctor. When we are sick or injured in an accident we immediately go to the hospital. We even call specialists to transport us to the hospital. This indicates that when it comes to medicine we believe in the scientific method and the various scientific disciplines that inform medicine — chemistry, biology, physics, etc. When scientists, however, tell us that we are dangerously warming the planet and that we are at the edge of a catastrophe through our burning of fossil fuels, a part of the population somehow feels at liberty to say that they do not believe it. When it comes to climate change some seem to feel as if we are at liberty to deny belief in the various scientific disciplines that inform climate science — chemistry, biology, physics, etc. When the swine flu broke out last spring and there was a real concern of a deadly pandemic, the press and people turned to the United States Center for Disease Control for information. We watched and listened to the experts to try to understand the outbreak and take preventative measures to avoid being infected. Since the outbreak of the swine flu I have never heard anyone ask: Do you believe in swine flu? If someone said, in intelligent company, that they did not believe that the flu could pass from a pig to a person, they would be laughed at. But when it comes to global warming, it is common for people to say, "I don't believe in global warming," or, "I do not believe that human beings are causing global warming." To some people that seems to be all right, to be intellectually responsible. It is, however, enormously irresponsible and dangerous.

The central question is not whether one believes in global warming. The central question is whether one believes in science and the scientific method. If you believe in or accept the scientific method, which all of us implicitly do when we go to a hospital when we are sick, then you have to accept that human beings are warming the planet through the burning of fossil fuels. Unless one is a Ph.D. who specializes in climate science and has some alternative theory as to the present warming of the climate, one is acting irresponsibly when one denies global warming, for the scientific consensus that human beings are dangerously warming the planet is overwhelming. The most prestigious scientific bodies in the world have all issued public statements that global warming is real and is caused mainly by human beings. This includes the National Academy of Sciences of the United States, the United Kingdom, France, Germany, Italy, Japan, Mexico, South Africa, China, India, and Russia.[6] This is "also the overwhelming majority view among the faculty members of the earth sciences departments at every first-rank university in the world."[7] The most prestigious scientific institutions in the United States across all the relevant disciplines hold this thesis: the American Association for the Advancement of Science, the National Research Council, the American Society of Microbiology, the American Geophysical Union, the American Meteorological Society, the American Institute of Physics. Indeed, eighteen of the leading relevant scientific organizations in the United States recently wrote a letter to the U.S. Senate telling them that it is unequivocal that climate change is occurring, that ongoing climate change "will have broad impacts on society, including the global economy and the environment," that "the severity of climate change impacts is expected to increase substantially in the coming decades," and that "if we are to avoid the most severe impacts of climate change, emissions of greenhouse gases must be dramatically reduced."[8] In addition, the Intergovernmental Panel on Climate Change has released a series of reports providing a summary of the scientific consensus that global warming is real, is caused mainly by human beings, and will result in very severe impacts for society. The IPCC Fourth Assessment is the consensus of 1200 authors and 2500 scientific expert reviewers from more than 130 countries. In addition, over 100 governments participated in the review process, making this report arguably "the most extensively peer reviewed science document in history."[9]

Second, while the first reason that there is a gap between the relevant scientific communities' assessment of the global warming problem and the public awareness of the problem is that most Americans do not experience the effects of climate change, the second reason is the well-known and widely documented fact that oil and coal companies have been funding institutes that spread disinformation regarding global warming. Company records of the world's second largest company, ExxonMobil, show that it has been funding global warming denial groups, for years. Exxon has admitted that it has been doing this, yet, despite its pledge in 2008 to no longer fund these groups Exxon has continued to fund denial groups like the National Center for Policy Analysis in Dallas and the Heritage Foundation in Washington, D.C. The coal industry has given millions to lobbying groups, purportedly $40 million to American Coalition for Clean Coal Electricity (ACCCE), whose slick ad campaigns lead us to believe that coal is clean so that we can burn coal now without increasing carbon dioxide emissions despite the fact that there is no successful commercial-scale clean coal plant in the world.[10] This corporate money and the lobbying groups also influence Congress and the politics of climate change.

Third, the climate issue has been turned into a partisan political dispute in the United States. People who do not know the science but trust their respective party leaders get their disinformation from the party leaders. Former President George W. Bush, for most of his two terms, censored James Hansen of NASA, the most prestigious climate scientist in the world, while inviting into the White House a science fiction writer, Michael Crichton, to present his case against the reality of global warming. James Inhofe, the chairman of the Senate Committee on the Environment and Public Works from 2003 to 2007, and the second largest recipient of campaign money from the oil industry, called catastrophic global warming the greatest hoax ever perpetrated on the American people.[11] He remains the ranking Republican on the committee. Treating global warming as a partisan political issue is largely an American phenomenon. In England, for instance, Conservative Prime Minister Margaret Thatcher established the Hadley Center in 1990 because of her concern about the threat of global warming. The Hadley Center is now one of the most important centers in the world for climate research.

Fourth, the press, which could have been a strong corrective to the disinformation campaigns, has done a poor job of communicating what is at stake and providing accurate information for the public. While a Kalb Fellow at Harvard's prestigious Joan Shorenstein Center on the Press, Politics, and Public Policy, a leading American journalist, Eric Pooley, has written a devastating critique of the media's coverage of global warming, especially the economics of climate change.[12] His analysis of

> news articles published in national and regional newspapers, wire services, and newsmagazines between December 2007 and June 2008 suggests that for most reporters covering this story, the default role was that of stenographer — presenting a nominally balanced view of the debate without questioning the validity of the arguments, sometimes even ignoring evidence that one side was twisting truth.... The media's collective decision to play the stenographer role actually helped opponents of climate action stifle progress.... Editors failed to devote sufficient resources to the climate story. In general, global warming is still being shoved into the "environment" pigeonhole, along with the spotted owls and delta smelt, when it is clearly to society's detriment to think about the subject that way. It is time for editors to treat climate policy as a permanent, important beat: tracking a mobilization for the moral equivalent of war.[13]

Furthermore, he concluded,

> the central problem... is the choice news organizations have made not to devote the necessary manpower and column inches to the climate policy story. Top editors need to decide that this will no longer be a disposable beat. Until that happens, the press will continue to underreport the story of the

century: the race to save the planet from a meteor known as humankind.[14]

Climate Change Impacts

We are already going to experience big impacts from global warming. If we delay much longer we run the risk of truly catastrophic impacts.

Right now the world is in a race (and I want to underscore "race" here) to hold global warming to a 2 degree Celsius (3.6 degrees Fahrenheit) increase above temperatures at the dawn of the industrial revolution. According to the Intergovernmental Panel on Climate Change (IPCC) this requires keeping atmospheric carbon dioxide concentrations below 450 parts per million. Right now we are at 385 ppm. At the current rate of emissions we will reach 450 ppm by 2030.[15] Even if we do not go over 450 ppm of CO_2 in the atmosphere, we still run the risk of experiencing some serious effects.

A seminal study from the National Oceanic and Atmospheric Administration (NOAA) shows that changes in surface temperature, rainfall, and sea level rise are largely irreversible for more than a thousand years after carbon dioxide (CO_2) emissions are completely stopped.[16] This means that if we completely stop emitting CO_2 today, some of the CO_2 in the atmosphere will linger for thousands of years and will continue to heat the planet. The study concludes: "among the illustrative irreversible impacts that should be expected if atmospheric carbon dioxide concentrations increase from current levels near 385 parts per million by volume (ppmv) to a peak of 450–600 ppmv over the coming century are irreversible dry-season rainfall reductions in several regions comparable to those of the 'dust bowl' era and inexorable sea level rise."[17] This study says that even if we manage to keep CO_2 to 450 ppm, we are running the risk of transforming the American West into a permanent dust bowl. In the worst years of the dustbowl in the U.S. "millions of acres of Great Plains topsoil blew all the way to Chicago, dumping red snow on New England. Hundreds of thousands of people, including 85 percent of Oklahoma's entire population, left the land."[18] Another study published in the journal *Climatic Change* draws upon data from the earth's history to show that six thousand years ago the U.S. High Plains were 1 to 2 degrees Celsius warmer than today (i.e., 2004) during the summer growing season months of June, July, and August.[19] At this time the Sand Hills of Nebraska really were sand hills. They were, according to Mark Lynas, "part of an immense system of sand dunes that spread across thousands of miles of the Great Plains, from Texas and Oklahoma in the south, right through Kansas, Colorado, Wyoming, North and South Dakota, to as far north as the Canadian prairie states of Saskatchewan and Manitoba."[20]

Just imagine the economic and social consequences of turning the western part of the United States into a dustbowl for at least a thousand years? But it will not just be the United States; other areas that will be turned into permanent dust bowls will be southern Europe, northern Africa, southern Africa, and western Australia. This study indicates that we are on the cusp of irreversibly changing the planet. Michael Oppenheimer, a member of the IPCC and professor of geosciences at Princeton University, responded to the recent study by saying, "Policy makers need to understand that in some ways once we are over the cliff, there's nothing to stop the fall."[21]

On June 16, 2009, the long awaited ten-year interagency report from the U.S. Global Change Research Program (USGCRP) was released. The report, *Global Climate Change Impacts in the United States,* and accompanying website are the most comprehensive assessment of the future effects of climate change in the United States. The report says, "the projected rapid rate and large amount of climate change over this century will challenge the ability of society and natural systems to adapt."[22]

We are currently emitting more greenhouse gases than the highest emissions scenario developed by the Intergovernmental Panel on Climate Change (IPCC).[23] The report by the U.S. Global Change Research Program (USGCRP) on climate change impacts in the United States maintains that by the end of the century, on the higher emissions scenario, "the average U.S. temperature is projected to increase by approximately 7 to 11 degrees Fahrenheit [as compared to the average temperature from 1961 to 1979]."[24] Kansas City, along with most of Kansas and the northern half of Missouri, will be at least 11 degrees Fahrenheit hotter in the summer. Let me put these average temperatures increases in perspective. For those of us who are used to 30 degree temperature swings in a day, this does

not seem like a big deal. When you talk about average temperature and thus move from weather to climate, this is a very big deal.
For instance, at the peak of the last ice age the average temperature
of the earth was 11 degrees Fahrenheit cooler and the higher latitudes of North America were covered with glaciers that were up
to 2.5 miles thick. On our current emissions path we are moving
in the opposite direction toward warming the earth by 11 degrees
Fahrenheit.

The study further predicts that Kansas City will have 105 to 120
days a year (3.5 to 4 months) with temperatures above 90 degrees.[25]
Western Kansas and southern Missouri, just south of Kansas City,
will have 120 days a year above 90 degrees. Southern California,
southern Arizona, south Texas, and south Florida will have over
180 days a year (6 months) above 90 degrees Fahrenheit. Furthermore, extreme heat events that now occur once every twenty years
will happen in Kansas City every other year. For the whole western part of the United States extreme heat events will occur every
year.[26] To try to put these temperature increases in perspective the
report focuses on the 2003 heat wave in Europe that killed 52,000
people.[27] The report says, "If greenhouse gas emissions continue to
increase, by the 2040s more than half of European summers will be
hotter than the summer of 2003, and by the end of the century, a
summer as hot as that of 2003 will be considered unusually cool."[28]

High temperatures can be deadly, especially for the elderly, but
they can also "diminish crop yields, melt mountain glaciers that
feed the earth's rivers, cause more destructive storms, increase the
area affected by drought, and cause more frequent and destructive
wildfires."[29]

I will not treat all of these effects; rather, I will focus on how
global warming is predicted to affect our food and water supplies.
It is important to remember that agriculture as we know it has
developed over the last eleven thousand years in a relatively stable
climate. We are now moving beyond the average mean temperature
range in which agriculture has developed. If we compare the afore-
mentioned projected temperature increases and number of days
above 90 degrees to the temperature range in which our most important grains grow, then it becomes evident that our grain supply is
at risk in a warming world. The optimum temperature for corn to
pollinate is 70 degrees. At 95 degrees during the pollination period

corn does not pollinate and you have a crop failure. The optimum temperature for the growth of corn is 80 degrees; at 102 degrees photosynthesis breaks down resulting in greatly diminished yields. This same pattern is evident in soy and in other important grains like wheat and rice.[30] A study conducted in the Philippines by the International Rice Research Institute (IRRI), which has been confirmed by other studies, and published by the U.S. National Academy of Sciences in 2004, argues that for every 1 degree Celsius (1.8 degree Fahrenheit) rise above the norm, wheat, rice, and corn yields fall by 10 percent.[31] We are in a race to stay under a 2 degree Celsius increase. On this analysis, even if we are able to stabilize average global temperature at a 2 degree Celsius increase, we are still looking at a 20 percent reduction in grain yields. A new study in the Proceedings of the National Academy of Sciences has found that "yields increase with temperature up to 29 degrees [84 degrees Fahrenheit] for corn, 30 degrees [86 degrees Fahrenheit] for soybeans, and 32 degrees Centigrade [89.6 degrees Fahrenheit] for cotton but that temperatures above these thresholds are very harmful."[32] The study concluded, based on current growing regions, that on the slowest of the IPCC warming scenarios (i.e., scenario B1), in which CO_2 is stabilized at around 560 ppm, corn and soy "yields are predicted to decrease by 30–46 percent before the end of the century."[33] On the highest and most rapid warming scenario (i.e., scenario A1F1) corn and soy yields are predicted to decrease by 63–82 percent. Again, it is important to keep in mind that we are currently emitting more greenhouse gases than the highest emissions scenario (i.e., scenario A1F1) of the IPCC.[34] This study also raised the question of our ability to adapt our grain crops to high temperatures. It looked at cotton to see if farmers in the warmer south had adapted (e.g., by developing heat resistant seeds for cotton) to frequent days of high heat (i.e., above 29 degrees Centigrade or 84 degrees Fahrenheit). They discovered that even though farmers in the south have experienced more extreme temperatures more often than those in the north, they had not been any more successful than farmers in the north at mitigating the negative effects of these high temperatures. This does not mean that heat resistant crops cannot be developed in the future, but at this point it is uncertain that they can be developed.[35] It is important to realize, as this study points out, that "the United States produces 41 percent of the world's corn and 38 percent of the world's soybeans. These crops comprise two of the four largest sources of caloric energy produced and are thus critical for world food supply."[36] While higher heat during the growing season is likely to sharply reduce crop yields, 70 million more children are born into the world every year so that by 2030 the population is likely to increase from over 6 billion today to 8 billion. As more and more people in the developing world emerge from poverty (e.g., in China) they tend to move from simple grain diets to more complex diets that include meat and dairy, which require a large quantity of grains to produce. As a result, the demand for food by 2030 is predicted to increase by 50 percent.[37] These converging factors only strengthen the International Rice Research Institute's (IRRI) contention from its 2004 study that "temperature increases due to global warming will make it increasingly difficult to feed Earth's growing population."[38]

Higher temperatures require plants to use more water, but higher temperatures also lead to drought and less available water. As global warming dries out the land it also threatens nature's fresh water reservoirs. Glaciers, snow, and ice masses in the mountains act as giant water towers. During the wet season precipitation in the mountains comes in the form of snow. The snow and ice that builds up in the wet season releases water during the hot dry season. Half of the world's 6.76 billion people depend on rivers whose freshwater source is mountain glaciers.[39] The Hindu Kush-Himalayan-Tibetan plateau glaciers, which hold the largest ice mass outside the polar regions, sustain seven of Asia's great river systems, providing fresh water for over a billion people in nearly every country in Asia. The historical observation record is less comprehensive for the Hindu Kush-Himalayan-Tibetan plateau as compared to some other glaciers around the world (e.g., the glaciers of the European Alps). Thus predictions are more uncertain for the Hindu Kush-Himalayan-Tibetan plateau. Recent studies maintain, however, that "the Tibetan glaciers have been melting at an accelerating, alarming rate over the past decade, raising the threat that many of the glaciers could be gone by midcentury."[40] This would leave 1.3 billion people short of water.

It is important to remember that 70 percent of our fresh water resources are used for irrigation of crops. Thus if you have water problems you are going to have food problems. During the dry season the glaciers of the Hindu Kush-Himalayan-Tibetan plateau sustain many irrigation systems. In Asia, the growing of wheat and rice depends upon these glaciers. The two largest wheat and rice producers in the world are China and India (the U.S. is the third largest wheat producer). China and India will be severely affected by the loss of these glaciers. Food will become more expensive everywhere in the world and, as always, the poor will be most severely impacted. Lester Brown, who is the founder of the World Watch Institute and the Earth Policy Institute, maintains that the projected melting of these glaciers "presents the most massive threat to food security humanity has ever faced."[41] This is not a scenario of the distant future. The melting of Himalayan glaciers is already happening faster than anyone thought possible and on our current path many of them could be gone by 2050: at that time my children will be in their forties.

The threat to the food supply is not only occurring on land, but also at sea. The oceans absorb more than 25 percent of the more than 29 billion tons of carbon dioxide that we pump into the atmosphere every year, and this causes the oceans to become more acidic. This acidity makes it more difficult for corals to form their skeletons. The Intergovernmental Panel on Climate Change maintains that the Great Barrier Reef, which is the world's largest living organism, "could be functionally extinct within decades."[42] This has enormous ramifications for ocean ecosystems and for human beings because "coral reefs provide significant protein supplies to about a billion people."[43] Not only does the acidification of the ocean affect corals but also plankton. According to Professor Ove Hoegh-Guldberg, who is a chief investigator at the ARC Centre of Excellence in Coral Reef Studies, "It isn't just the coral reefs which are affected — a large part of the plankton in the Southern Ocean, the coccolithophorids, are also affected. These drive ocean productivity and are at the base of the food web which supports krill, whales, tuna, and our fisheries. They also play a vital role in removing carbon dioxide from the atmosphere, which could break down."[44] According to the ARC Centre of Excellence, ocean acidity "could be lethal for . . . a third of the planet's marine life."[45] In short, we are threatening the foundations of the food web in the oceans. The Interacademy Panel on International Issues, in a statement that was endorsed by seventy national academies of science, including the U.S. National Academy of Science, maintains that the current rate of change in ocean chemistry from CO_2 is "much more rapid than during any event over the last 65 million years."[46] And the more rapid the change, the more difficult it is for species to adapt. Indeed, on our current emissions path we will reach 560 ppm of CO_2 in the atmosphere by 2050 and "the oceans will be more acidic than they have been for tens of millions of years."[47] Furthermore, events in Earth's geological history suggest that it will take tens of thousands of years for the ocean chemistry to recover "while the recovery of ecosystem function and biological diversity can take much longer."[48] Hoegh-Guldberg maintains, "When CO_2 levels in the atmosphere reach about 500 parts per million, you put calcification out of business in the oceans."[49] On our current emissions path we will hit 500 ppm in the 2040s: at that time my children will be in their thirties.

While the food web in the oceans will be threatened by acidification, the oceans will be rising. There is much that is unknown about the dynamics of ice sheets and there is much debate about the rate at which Greenland and west Antarctica can melt. The most recent estimates put the most likely sea level rise within the next ninety years at three to six feet.[50] The rising of the oceans and the increasing number of storm surges from a warmer ocean will also threaten our food supply. Even at the low end of present predictions, the rice harvests in Asia will be threatened. If the seas were to rise three feet, 50 percent of the rice fields in Bangladesh would be devastated by flooding. Bangladesh is home to 160 million people and it is projected to grow to over 250 million by 2050.[51] A three-foot sea level rise would wipe out "the rice harvest in the Mekong Delta, which produces more than half the rice in Viet Nam."[52] Vietnam is the world's second largest rice exporter. According to Lester Brown, "the fate of the hundreds of millions who depend on the harvests in the rice-growing river deltas and floodplains of Asia is inextricably linked to the fate of these major ice sheets."[53]

So we see that the face of climate change is not just the polar bears, but it is our face; it is the face of our children and our grandchildren. It is about food and water. It is about the survival of billions of people.

Throughout this account of the climate impacts on food and water supplies I have spoken of present observable trends and also about predictions. Climate sciences rely on three different sources: present observable data, data from the earth's history, and climate models. Now those of us who enjoy a good night's sleep might dismiss these predictions because climate models were involved in making them. Initially in my own reading I too sought refuge in this. The problem is that by every major indicator — Arctic sea ice, Greenland and Antarctica ice sheet melt, sea level rise, glacier melt, ocean acidification — climate change is coming faster than any of the models predicted. The rate of sea ice melt in the Arctic is thirty years ahead of the IPCC projections of 2007.[54] The IPCC models in 2001 projected that Greenland and Antarctica would gain mass until 2100 and then begin to melt. By 2006, it was clear that they were already losing mass. Richard Alley, a pioneering paleoclimatologist (i.e., an expert in the history of the earth's climate) and a member of the research team, responded to this new data by saying, "We're now 100 years ahead of schedule."[55] Actual sea level rise is 80 percent greater than was predicted by the 2001 and 2007 IPCC Reports.[56] The estimates of the maximum sea level rise by 2100 are now more than three times the maximum sea level estimates of the 2007 IPCC report.[57] Carbon dioxide pollution is raising ocean acidity ten to twenty times faster than previous models predicted.[58] Michael Oppenheimer, who is a member of the IPCC and professor of geosciences at Princeton University, in response to his own assessment of the models, succinctly described our present situation, "The more we learn about the problem, the more severe the risk becomes and the nearer it looms."[59]

It is well established that we are dangerously warming the planet; the uncertainty is around how quickly the climate system will change. In light of climate change already exceeding the models by every major indicator, this uncertainty is not at all comforting. The climate models are not only underestimating the present observable effects of warming, but they also underestimate what we know has taken place in the earth's history. Richard Alley evaluated the ability of the major climate models to simulate what is known to have happened in the earth's past. Alley showed in his review that the models underestimated what happened by over 30 percent.[60] Alley concluded, "If climate models are systematically underestimating reality, then the more radical-looking 'high side' of temperature projections may be more accurate than the conservative-looking 'low side.'"[61]

In light of evidence from the Earth's history and present observations of the rapid decline of Arctic sea ice, mountain glacier melt, Greenland and West Antarctica ice loss, the expansion of subtropical regions and arid regions around the world, and the negative responses of coral reefs (home to 25 percent of all marine species) to the warming of the oceans and to ocean acidification, Jim Hansen and a group of researchers published a paper that argues that the IPCC's target of limiting carbon dioxide in the atmosphere to 450 ppm is too high.[62] Thirty-four million years ago "Antarctica became cold enough to harbor a large ice sheet"[63] and carbon dioxide levels were at 450 ppm "with an estimated uncertainty, of 100 ppm."[64] Present observations, according to Hansen and his team, reduced this level of uncertainty allowing them to propose that 350 ppm was the upper limit of carbon dioxide levels. If the end-of-summer Arctic sea ice was declining so quickly and "Greenland and West Antarctica were each losing mass at more than 100 cubic kilometers per year,"[65] then "clearly the ice sheets are unstable with the present climate forcing"[66] of 385 ppm. According to Hansen, "if humanity burns most of the fossil fuels, doubling [560 ppm] or tripling [840 ppm] the preindustrial carbon dioxide level [280 ppm], Earth will surely head toward the ice free condition, with sea level 75 meters (250 feet) higher than today."[67] You do not just wake up and find that sea level has changed 250 feet. While the ultimate effect is unimaginably devastating for human civilization, this time lag has its own devastating component. What would it mean for our globalized society if there were no stable coastlines for centuries? What would it mean for civilization if the sea level rose three feet every twenty to twenty-five years (twelve to fifteen feet a century) for centuries as it did at the end of the last ice age fourteen thousand years ago?[68] Even, "a 1 to 2 meter [3 to 6 feet] sea level rise would be disastrous for hundreds of millions of people."[69] The "ramifications of a major sea level rise are massive, agriculture will be disrupted, water supplies will be salinized, storms and flood waters will reach ever further inland, and millions of environmental refugees will be created — 15 million people live at or below three feet elevation in Bangladesh, for example. Governments, especially those in the developing world, will be disrupted, creating political instability."[70] A three-foot sea level rise "would flood all of Miami Beach and leave downtown Miami sitting as an island of water, disconnected from the rest of Florida."[71] Other major U.S. cities that would be severely impacted by a three-foot sea level rise include New York, Newark, New Orleans, Boston, Washington, Philadelphia, Tampa-St. Petersburg, and San Francisco. The most threatened major cities outside North America include Osaka, Kobe, Nagoya, and Tokyo in Japan and Rotterdam and Amsterdam in the Netherlands.[72] In light of these effects from a three-foot sea level rise, imagine the seas rising three feet every twenty to twenty-five years for centuries up to 250 feet.

According to Hansen and these other researchers, "If humanity wishes to preserve a planet similar to that on which civilization developed and to which life on Earth has adapted, paleoclimate evidence [i.e., the Earth's history] and ongoing climate change suggest that CO_2 will need to be reduced from its current 385 ppm to at most 350 ppm, but likely less than that.... If the present overshoot of this target $C0_2$ is not brief, there is a possibility of seeding irreversible catastrophic effects."[73] According to Hansen's analysis we have to reduce CO_2 to 350 ppm by the end of the century. This can be done by stopping all coal burning in the next twenty years and drawing down CO_2 through a variety of agricultural practices. If CO_2 concentrations get too high, we will be unable to draw down the CO_2. Hansen has to be taken very seriously because he has been out in front of the scientific community for thirty years. Indeed, he has predicted most of what has happened to the climate over the past thirty years.[74]

All this is worrisome enough. There is, however, an elephant in the room that is not well known by the public, namely, that the historical climate record shows that abrupt climate change is the norm, not the exception. In its 2001 report, the IPCC said "abrupt climate change is an issue that haunts the climate change problem."[75] According to the report from the U.S. National Academy of Sciences in 2002, "recent scientific evidence shows that major and widespread climate changes have occurred with startling speed.... The new paradigm of an abruptly changing climate system has been well established by research over the last decade, but this new thinking is little known and scarcely appreciated in the wider community of natural and social scientists and policymakers."[76] Richard Alley, who was chair of the U.S. National Academy of Sciences Committee on Abrupt Climate Change, and his co-researchers have discovered that when the Earth emerged from the last ice age around eleven thousand years ago the world warmed by at least 9 degrees Fahrenheit in ten years.[77] This is roughly the 2007 IPCC report's prediction for where we will be at the end of this century on our business-as-usual emissions path.

In response to this uncertainty about where the thresholds are for abrupt climate change, Pieter Tans of the National Oceanic and Atmospheric Administration said in an interview, "Basically, we are playing Russian roulette, with the revolver pointed at the generation of our children and grandchildren."[78] Wallace Broecker, one of the pioneers in the discovery of abrupt climate change, in an influential piece in *Nature* commented on the historical record of such abrupt climate change and our response to the problem: "To date, we have dealt with this problem as if its effects would come in the distant future and so gradually that we could easily cope with them. This is certainly a possibility, but I believe that there is an equal possibility that they will arrive suddenly and dramatically. . . . [79] We play Russian roulette with climate, hoping that the future will hold no unpleasant surprises. No one knows what lies in the active chamber of the gun, but I am less optimistic about its contents than many."[80]

The National Academy of Sciences report on abrupt climate change maintains that the more rapidly we push the climate system "the more likely it is that the resulting change will be abrupt on the timescale of human economies or global ecosystems."[81] A study published last year in the journal *Nature Geosciences* shows that we are putting CO_2 into the atmosphere fourteen thousand times faster than nature has over the past six hundred thousand years.[82]

The Global Warming Gamble: Taking Unimaginable Risks

There has been great public outcry this year about Wall Street traders and executives receiving bonuses after their reckless risk taking collapsed the financial system. The airwaves have been filled with condemnation about how outrageously unjust it is that the people responsible for the problem walked away with millions in taxpayer bailout money and left us to pay for and clean up after their mess. Are we not, however, doing this on the grandest of scales? Climate scientists are saying in the strongest possible terms that we are pushing the climate system to the brink and that it is susceptible to a crash, to a great reversal. We are taking the greatest of gambles with our children's and our grandchildren's futures — indeed, the future of the next fifty generations. Most especially, we are running the risk of condemning the poorest of the world, the 2.6 billion people who survive on less than $2 a day, to a desperate struggle for food and water and all the displacement, violence, and suffering that such a struggle could entail. We are creating conditions for death and destruction on an unimaginable scale. While the planet's population is projected to reach 9 billion by 2050, Hans Joachim Schellenhuber, one of the leading climate scientists in the world, carefully argued at a major international climate conference that at a 5 degree Celsius (9 degrees Fahrenheit) increase from pre-industrial temperatures, which is where we are headed on our current path, the planet could probably support only about 1 billion people.[83] To have even a faint sense of what these statistics mean one must recognize that they conceal as much as they reveal. We can only begin to imagine the enormity of the tragedy we are risking if we move from these statistics to the recognition that each stroke in this tally represents a life: a particular human being, a son or daughter, a husband or wife, father or mother.

While the financial sector can be bailed out by taxpayer money in order to avoid a great depression, Mother Nature does not accept bailouts. Nature is just chemical, biological, and physical processes operating according to their own laws and their own timetable. In the words of Michael Oppenheimer, "Once we are over the cliff, there's nothing to stop the fall."[84]

Those who contributed nothing (future generations) or virtually nothing to the problem (the world's poor) will experience the greatest consequences. The richest 7 percent of the world's population are responsible for 50 percent of the world's carbon dioxide emissions, while the poorest 50 percent of the world's population have contributed just 7 percent of the world's carbon dioxide emissions.[85] The United States has a particular responsibility. It is true that China recently surpassed the United States as the largest carbon dioxide polluter in the world. China produced 22 percent of world carbon dioxide emissions in 2008, the United States produced 17.9 percent, followed by India at 5.5 percent.[86] This, however, is not the central issue. Since carbon dioxide that is not absorbed by oceans or land, especially vegetation, lasts a thousand years in the atmosphere, the central statistic is cumulative historical emissions. On this score, the United States has emitted three times as much carbon dioxide as any other country. The U.S. is responsible for 27 percent of emissions from 1750 to 2008, followed by China at 9 percent, and India, which is further down in these rankings, is responsible for 2.7 percent of emissions.[87]

The Potential of Renewable Energy Sources

The risks to which we are subjecting ourselves and our children are not a matter of necessity; they are a matter of choice. The choice is not between burning fossil fuels to run our advanced society or going back to the Stone Age. The earth has an abundance of energy resources. While the climate system can shift quickly, the resources are available for us to shift quickly. The public is not only uninformed about the threat of global warming but also about the potential for change. There is much more solar, geothermal, and wind energy available to us than we need.

Enough solar energy hits the earth's surface in forty minutes to power the entire world for a year. A Department of Energy report to Congress in 2007 showed that the U.S. Southwest has some of the best solar energy resources in the world. There is enough harnessable solar power in the Southwest through concentrated solar power to meet nearly seven times the electricity needs of the entire country.[88] There are two kinds of solar power: photovoltaic and concentrated. Photovoltaic solar power consists of panels that convert the sun's energy into electricity. Concentrated solar power uses hundreds of mirrors to concentrate the sun's power onto a tower containing oil or molten salts, which then heat up water to drive a steam turbine and generate electricity. Those plants that use a molten salts solution can store power up to six hours after sun down and the technology to store power so that you have power twenty-four hours a day is not far off. These plants can be built very quickly — in two or three years — and they use very little water because they can be air-cooled.[89] Within a few years, certainly before 2013, the cost to consumers could be less than nuclear plants and coal plants with carbon capture and storage.[90] If we covered the equivalent of a ninety-two-by-ninety-two mile square grid in the Southwest with concentrated solar power arrays we could generate enough electricity for the entire United States.[91] We would, however, have to invest in a national smart grid to distribute this energy from the deserts of the Southwest to the rest of the United States. Other parts of the world also have huge solar resources including Mexico, southern Europe, North Africa, the Middle East, China, India, Pakistan, and Australia.[92]

Not only can we draw upon energy from the sun, but we can also draw upon energy from the earth — geothermal energy. The heat in the upper six miles of the earth's crust contains around fifty thousand times more energy than all the world's oil and gas reserves combined.[93] Oil and gas companies already have the technology to drill down over six miles. We could use that technology to tap into the earth's energy and generate power twenty-four hours a day seven days a week without any carbon emissions.

Wind energy is also plentiful. A 1991 Department of Energy study asserted that North Dakota, Kansas, and Texas had enough harnessable wind energy to satisfy national electricity needs.[94] With the latest technology, wind power could satisfy not only our electricity needs but all our energy needs. A 2005 Department of Energy assessment of offshore wind energy concluded that U.S. offshore wind out to a distance of fifty miles alone is sufficient to meet 70 percent of national electricity needs.[95] A 2005 study in the *Journal of Geophysical Research* concludes that harnessing only 20 percent of the earth's available wind energy would provide seven times the electricity that the world currently uses.[96] China has enough wind energy to double its current electrical generating capacity.[97]

The cost savings of rapidly moving to renewable energies are quite high. A recent study from Stanford University and the University of California Davis demonstrates that if the world moved entirely to renewable sources of energy (this does not include nuclear power) by 2030 this would reduce worldwide power demand by 30 percent and replace the need for thirteen thousand new or existing coal plants. According to this study's analysis of only land locations, thus excluding offshore locations, with a high potential for producing power, wind energy has the potential to produce five to fifteen times the power needed to power the whole world. Similarly, solar energy could produce thirty times the power needed for the entire world. Building all the solar, wind, geothermal, and hydropower infrastructure along with all the transmission lines to carry this power would still yield a long-run net savings that would more than equal the costs.[98]

Perhaps the quickest way to reduce carbon dioxide emissions is through energy efficiency. According to a study by the McKinsey Global Institute the United States can reduce emissions 40 percent by 2030 through energy efficiency alone.[99]

Political Will and the Power of the Public

We have all the resources available with existing technology or technology that is already in development to pull back from the brink of the climate catastrophe. The problem is not scarcity of resources; it is political will. The big coal and oil companies have the capital and capacity to switch to renewable forms of energy. They, however, have poured millions of dollars into Congress and disinformation campaigns over the last twelve years to keep us hooked on fossil fuels. As it has become increasingly clear that the world is headed toward renewable energy in the long term, these companies are pouring millions of dollars into lobbying Congress to assure that the transition to renewable energy allows them to get as much as possible out of their existing investment in fossil fuels and thus maximize their profits. The danger is that we will continue to allow the pace of response to our critical situation to be dictated by a time frame established by the fossil fuel companies, not the time frame of nature.

We have the human resources to change the politics of this problem. The common perception that we are helpless in the face of big industry and its influence on Congress is not true. In response to the beaches of Santa Barbara, California, being contaminated from an oil spill and the pollution in the Cuyahoga River in Ohio catching on fire, 20 million Americans, which was 10 percent of the population at the time, took to the streets during the first Earth Day in April 1970. Because of these demonstrations the Environmental

Protection Agency was formed, and the Clean Air Act and the Clean Water Act were passed by 1972 under President Richard Nixon.

A more recent example of the considerable power of the public is also instructive. On Saturday March 14, 2009, it was reported that American International Group (A.I.G.), the failed insurance company that was bailed out by American taxpayers, awarded $165 million in bonuses to its employees, including those in the financial products unit that was at the center of the financial systems near collapse.[100] The American people were so outraged by this injustice that they flooded the phone lines of Congress complaining about the bonuses paid to A.I.G. employees with taxpayer money.[101] By Tuesday, March 17, within one business day, congressional leaders were devising ways to get the bonus money returned. And by Thursday March 19 the House of Representatives overwhelmingly passed a 90 percent tax on bonuses to employees of A.I.G. and other firms that received large amounts of federal bailout money.[102] These examples are a clear indication that the American public has an enormous amount of power when it makes its voice heard en masse.

The Internet and the communication technology we have has given us unprecedented power to come together to fight the incredible climate injustice. Indeed, there has never been a time in the history of world when people could so easily organize and mobilize for a cause. We have the capacity to organize and mobilize to pressure our political leaders to follow the timetable of nature, not the timetable of big coal and big oil. Yet we are asleep. We are not using this technology to save our future; rather, it is often used to entertain ourselves, to keep ourselves distracted, to keep ourselves asleep. Each passing day provides a host of new celebrity sex scandals, new political spectacles, the death of pop stars and fashion models and the press fills up our media with these trivialities. And we tune in day after day and week after week and all the while Greenland is melting, the Arctic sea ice is disappearing, the glaciers are melting, the ocean is being poisoned, and the survival of billions of people is at stake. And while we sleep and use our technology to stay entertained big coal and big oil are in the halls of Congress gambling away our children's future. This is the unimaginable tragedy that is unfolding.

What Should We Do?
Some Concrete Proposals

We need to wake up and speak out today, tomorrow, and for the foreseeable future. For, as Steven Chu, the U.S. secretary of energy and Nobel Prize winner has said, "From here on in, every day has to be Earth Day."[103] But what concretely needs to be done? Though this question will be treated in depth in the last essay in this volume, I would like to put forward some concrete suggestions for consideration.

First, we need to push for laws that will require our economy and markets to tell the truth about the burning of fossil fuels. Nicholas Stern, who was the chief economist of the World Bank from 2000 to 2003 and author of the *Stern Review* on the economics of climate change, has said that "climate change is the result of the greatest market failure the world has seen,"[104] because the markets do not tell the real truth about carbon. The true cost of carbon is not factored into the markets. For instance, the market considers coal to be cheap, but the enormous untold costs of pollution from burning coal are simply passed on to future generations.

The legislation that passed through the House of Representatives in July 2009 (the American Clean Energy and Security Act) and the bill introduced in the Senate (the Clean Energy Jobs and American Power Act), which is scheduled to be voted on in the spring of 2010, will begin to tell the truth about carbon. The House bill was a great political achievement by its sponsors — Henry Waxman and Edward Markey. The problem with both of these bills, however, is that they are not in line with the science. To have a likely chance of not exceeding a 2 degree Celsius warming from pre-industrial times, global carbon dioxide emissions need to fall 50 to 80 percent below the 1990 level by 2050. Up to 2050 the developed world needs to cut its emissions more than the developing world. The congressional bills are in line with the 2050 target of an 80 percent reduction in CO_2 emissions, but they are not in line with the 2020 target of cutting carbon dioxide emissions 40 percent below 1990 levels.[105] The bills in Congress call for carbon dioxide emissions to be reduced around 3 percent below 1990 levels by 2020. By delaying deep cuts, this makes it significantly more difficult to meet the 2050 target.[106] The Unites States, however, must pass a bill and get a framework in place; any further delay would be disastrous. The original Clean Air Act did not do enough to reduce airborne pollutants, and the original Montreal Protocol did not do enough to stop the destruction of the ozone layer from ozone depleting substances. Both of these, however, began a process and built a framework that was strengthened over time to accomplish the particular task. The hope is that while the climate targets of the congressional bills are insufficient they can be strengthened over time to meet the challenge.

Second, if the climate legislation is passed, then strengthening it over time will probably require the public to demand that their congressional leaders follow the science. One way this can happen is through educating, organizing, and mobilizing fellow Catholics. This can be done through establishing in one's parish, school, or university a Catholic Climate Covenant group. This group could draw upon the resources provided at the Catholic Climate Covenant[107] and the Catholic Coalition on Climate Change.[108] Such a group could also become involved with other organizations that have developed many tools to educate, organize, and mobilize people. The Earth Policy Institute[109] provides in-depth up-to-date information including a PowerPoint presentation for educational purposes.[110] The We Campaign[111] is probably the largest group, with over 5 million members working to educate, organize, and mobilize people to become politically active on the climate issue. The We Campaign sends out action notices alerting members to contact their congressional leaders when important legislation is being considered in Congress. In addition, it has tools that allow one to contact one's congressional leaders and even has online functions that facilitate writing a letter to the editors of national and local newspapers.[112] All of these functions make it easy to become politically active on the climate issue.

Third, Catholics should also become involved in the growing national movement to stop the building of coal-fired power plants. Guided by the science, environmental groups, especially the Sierra Club, have mobilized and pushed for a moratorium on new coal-fired power plants. From May 2007 to December 19, 2009, the efforts of grassroots campaigns has led to 112 of the 228 proposed coal plant projects to be canceled and the future of 31 has become uncertain.[113] This is a major success that Catholics should support.

Fourth, in December 2009 the much anticipated United Nations Climate Change Conference in Copenhagen failed to put in place a framework for a binding international agreement to limit global warming to a 2 degree Celsius increase above pre-industrial levels. The Copenhagen Conference ended with an accord that aspires to the 2 degrees Celsius limit, but did not clearly show how that target would be achieved. Several assessments by climate scientists predict that if the emission reduction commitments and pledges put forward by developed and developing countries were realized, then the world would still be headed to an increase of 3.5 degree Celsius, with CO_2 levels above 650 ppm, to an increase of 3.9 degree Celsius, with CO_2 levels at 780 ppm, increase above pre-industrial levels.[114] As this essay, has made painfully clear, such an increase in CO_2 levels would be catastrophic for the human community, especially for the poor in the developing world.

In light of this, I have become convinced that people need to start demonstrating en masse in the streets all across the globe, especially in the United States. This is already starting to happen. One group that is particularly promising is 350.org (*www.350.org*), which organized an international day of climate action on October 24, 2009, which included 5200 events in 181 countries. Catholic Climate Covenant groups in parishes, schools, and universities could participate in 350.org events. Parish and school groups could also team up with other parishes and schools in a diocese to organize walks for climate justice that would take the popular format of walking for a cause (e.g., "The Walk for Hope to Cure Breast Cancer") and adapt it to the climate issue (e.g., "Walk for Climate Justice" or "Walk for Our Children's Future"). And maybe as Catholics become more knowledgable of the climate problem and its implications, they just might find themselves following in the footsteps of James Hansen, who is now participating in protests at coal-fired power plants.

Whatever the particular course of action, an individual or group finally decides upon in response to the climate crisis, the questions that should permeate Catholic parishes, schools, and universities, in forming their consciences on the climate issue, are the questions forcefully posed by Pope Benedict XVI in his 2010 World Day of Peace Message "If You Want to Cultivate Peace, Protect Creation":

Can we remain indifferent before the problems associated with such realities as climate change, desertification, the deterioration and loss of productivity in vast agricultural areas, the pollution of rivers and aquifers, the loss of biodiversity, the increase of natural catastrophes and the deforestation of equatorial and tropical regions? Can we disregard the growing phenomenon of "environmental refugees," people who are forced by the degradation of their natural habitat to forsake it — and often their possessions as well — in order to face the dangers and uncertainties of forced displacement? Can we remain impassive in the face of actual and potential conflicts involving access to natural resources?[115]

Notes

1. James Hansen, "Global Warming Twenty Years Later: Tipping Points Near" (June 23, 2008), 1. *www.columbia.edu/~jeh1/2008/TwentyYearsLater_20080623.pdf*. This is the text of a presentation Hansen gave to the National Press Club and to the House Select Committee on Energy Independence & Global Warming.

2. Peter T. Doran and Maggie Kendall Zimmerman, "Examining the Scientific Consensus on Climate Change," *EOS, Transaction American Geophysical Union* 90, no. 3 (2009): 22–23. *EOS* is available only to American Geophysical Union members, but Professor Doran has provided public access to the article through a link on his website: *http://tigger.uic.edu/~pdoran/012009_Doran_final.pdf*.

3. James Hansen, "The Temperature of Science" (December 16, 2009), 3; online at *www.columbia.edu/~jeh1/mailings/2009/20091216_TemperatureOfScience.pdf*.

4. The National Oceanic and Atmospheric Association National Climatic Data Center, "State of the Climate Global Analysis: August 2009," see online *www.ncdc.noaa.gov/sotc/?report=global&year=2009&month=8&submitted=Get+Report* (accessed October 7, 2009).

5. Ibid., see the following graph, which is in Celsius: *www.ncdc.noaa.gov/sotc/get-file.php?report=global&file=map-blended-mntp&year=2009&month=8&ext=gif*.

6. See, for instance, the joint statement of the G8 National Academy of Sciences from May 2007, *www.nationalacademies.org/includes/G8Statement_Energy_07_May.pdf*.

7. John P. Holdren, "Convincing the Climate-Change Skeptics," *Boston Globe,* August 4, 2008.

8. American Association for the Advancement of Science, American Chemical Society, American Geophysical Union, American Institute of Biological Sciences, American Meteorological Society, American Society of Agronomy, American Society of Plant Biologists, American Statistical Association, Association of Ecosystem Research Centers, Botanical Society of America, Crop Science Society of America, Ecological Society of America, Natural Science Collections Alliance, Organizations of Biological Field Stations, Society for Industrial and Applied Mathematics, Society of Systematic Biologists, Soil Science Society of America, University Corporation for Atmospheric Research, "Letter to Senators" (October 21, 2009), *www.aaas.org/news/releases/2009/media/1021climate_letter.pdf*.

9. See the University of Oregon Institute for a Sustainable Environment, "Sources: *The 2007 Fourth Assessment Report of the Inter-governmental Panel on Climate Change*" at *http://climlead.uoregon.edu/node/78* (accessed January 5, 2010).

10. Kevin Grandia, "US Coal Industry Won't Give Up Easily on Using Atmosphere as a Dumping Ground," *Guardian,* August 19, 2009.

11. See the press release of Senator Inhofe, Monday July 28, 2003, *http://inhofe.senate.gov/pressapp/record.cfm?id=206907* (accessed on September 12, 2009).

12. Eric Pooley is a contributor for *Time* magazine. He has been managing editor of *Fortune,* editor of *Time Europe,* national editor of *Time, Time*'s chief political correspondent, and senior editor of *New York* magazine. In 1996, as *Time*'s White House correspondent, Pooley won the Gerald Ford Prize for Excellence in Reporting for his coverage of the Clinton administration.

13. Eric Pooley, "How Much Would You Pay to Save the Planet? The American Press and the Economics of Climate Change," Joan Shorenstein Center on the Press, Politics and Public Policy Discussion Paper Series #D-49, January 2009, 4–5, *www.hks.harvard.edu/presspol/publications/papers/discussion_papers/d49_pooley.pdf*.

14. Ibid, 20.

15. I. Allison, N. L. Bindoff, R. A. Bindoff, R. A. Bindschadler, P. M. Cox, N. de Noblet, M. H. England, J. E. Francis, N. Gruber, A. M. Haywood, D. J. Karoly, G. Kaser, C. Le Quéré, T. M. Lenton, M. E. Mann, B. I. McNeil, A. J. Pitman, S. Rahmstorf, E. Rignot, H. J. Schellenhuber, S. H. Schneider, S. C. Sherwood, R. C. J. Somerville, K. Steffen, E. J. Steig, M. Visbeck, A. J. Weaver, *The Copenhagen Diagnosis: Updating the World on the Latest Climate Science* (Sydney, Australia: University of New South Wales Climate Change Research Centre, 2009), 36.

16. Susan Solomon, Gian-Kasper Plattner, Reto Knutti, Pierre Fried-lingstein, "Irreversible Climate Change Due to Carbon Dioxide Emissions,"

PNAS 106, no. 6 (February 10, 2009): 1704–9. *www.pnas.org/content/early/2009/01/28/0812721106.full.pdf+ html.*

17. Ibid., 1704.

18. Mark Lynas, *Six Degrees: Our Future on a Hotter Planet* (Washington, D.C.: National Geographic Society, 2008), 30.

19. Jennifer M. Mangan, Jonathan T. Overpeck, Robert S. Webb, Carol Wessman, and Alexander F. H. Goetz. "Response of Nebraska Sand Hills Natural Vegetation to Drought, Fire, Grazing, and Plant Functional Type Shifts as Simulated by the Century Model," *Climatic Change* 63 (2004): 49–90 at 50.

20. Lynas, *Six Degrees,* 29.

21. Cornelia Dean, "Emissions Cut Won't Bring Quick Relief, Scientists Say," *New York Times,* January 27, 2009.

22. Thomas R. Karl, Jerry M. Melillo, and Thomas C. Peterson, eds., *Global Climate Change Impacts in the United States* (New York: Cambridge University Press, 2009), 10.

23. Ibid., 23.

24. Ibid., 29.

25. Ibid., 34.

26. Ibid., 33.

27. Janet Larsen, "Setting the Record Straight: More than 52,000 Europeans Died from Heat in Summer 2003," Earth Policy Institute: Plan B Updates (July 28, 2006). *www.earth-policy.org/index.php?/plan_b_updates/2006/update56.*

28. *Global Climate Change Impacts in the United States,* 24.

29. Lester R. Brown, *Plan B 3.0: Mobilizing to Save Civilization* (New York: W. W. Norton, 2008), 50.

30. The optimum temperature for soybeans to pollinate is 75 degrees; at 102 degrees during the pollination period you will have a crop failure. The optimum temperature for the growth of soybeans is 90 degrees; at 102 degrees corn stops growing.

31. Shaobing Pen et al., "Rice Yields Decline with Higher Night Temperature from Global Warming," PNAS 101, no. 27 (July 6, 2004): 9971–75.

32. Wolfram Schlenker and Michael J. Roberts, "Nonlinear Temperature Effects Indicate Severe Damages to U.S. Crop Yields Under Climate Change," PNAS 106, no. 37 (September 15, 2009): 15594–98 at 15594. *www.pnas.org/content/early/2009/08/25/0906865106.full.pdf+html.*

33. Ibid.

34. *Global Climate Change Impacts in the United States,* 23.

35. For a more accessible account of these finding see Michael J. Roberts's reflections on his article at *http://greedgreengrains.blogspot.com/ 2009/08/nonlinear-temperature-effects-indicate_27.html.*

36. Schlenker and Roberts, "Nonlinear Temperature Effects," 15594.

37. Sir John Beddington, "Speech at SDUK 09," *www.govnet.co.uk/ news/govnet/professor-sir-john-beddingtons-speech-at-sduk-09.* Sir John Beddington is the chief scientific adviser and head of the Government Office for Science in England. He was a professor of applied population biology at Imperial College London and is a fellow of the Royal Society.

38. Brown, *Plan B 3.0,* 53.

39. Thomas Kohler and Daniel Maselli, eds., *Mountains and Climate Change: From Understanding to Action* (Bern, Switzerland: Centre for Development and Environment, Institute of Geography, University of Bern, 2009), 12.

40. Baiqing Xu et al., "Black Soot and the Survival of Tibetan Glaciers," PNAS (published online before print edition, December 8, 2009), *www.pnas.org/content/early/2009/12/07/0910444106.full.pdf+html.*

41. Lester R. Brown, *Plan B 4.0: Mobilizing to Save Civilization* (New York: W. W. Norton, 2009), 6.

42. Bonnie Malkin, "Great Barrier Reef 'Will Die' Unless Carbon Emissions Slashed," *Telegraph,* November 17, 2009.

43. Beddington, "Speech at SDUK 09," 3.

44. ARC Centre of Excellence in Coral Reef Studies, "Acid Oceans Warning," News Updates and Media Releases, October 17, 2007, *www.coralcoe.org.au/news_stories/coralfutures.html* (accessed September 17, 2009).

45. Ibid.

46. The Interacademy Panel on International Issues, "IAP Statement on Ocean Acidification," June 2009, *www.interacademies.net/Object.File/ Master/9/075/Statement_RS1579_IAP_05.09final2.pdf.*

47. Ibid.

48. Ibid.

49. ARC Centre, "Acid Oceans Warning," *www.coralcoe.org.au/news _stories/coralfutures.html* (accessed September 17, 2009).

50. See Martin Vermeer and Stefan Rahmstorf, "Global Sea Level Linked to Global Temperature," PNAS 106, no. 51 (December 22, 2009): 21527–21532, *www.pnas.org/content/106/51/21527.full.pdf+html;* W. T. Pfeffer, J. T. Harper, and S. O'Neel, "Kinematic Constraints on Glacier Contributions to 21st Century Sea Level Rise," *Science* 321, no. 5894 (September 5, 2008): 1340–43, *www.sciencemag.org/cgi/ content/full/321/5894/1340;* for excellent images of sea level rise in different parts of the United States and the rest of the world see

www.geo.arizona.edu/dgesl/research/other/climate_change_and_sea_level/sea_level_rise/sea_level_rise_old.htm#images.

51. United States Agency for International Development/Bangladesh, "Bangladesh: Population & Health," *www.usaid.gov/bd/programs/pop_response.html.*

52. Brown, *Plan B 4.0: Mobilizing to Save Civilization,* 7.

53. Ibid.

54. J. Stroeve, M. Holland, M. Serreze, T. Scambos, "Arctic Sea Ice Decline: Faster Than Forecast?" *Geophysical Research Letters,* 34, L09501 (May 1, 2007).

55. Peter N. Spotts, "Little Time to Avoid the Big Thaw, Scientists Warn: Arctic Temperatures Near a Prehistoric Level When Seas Were 16 to 20 Feet Higher, Studies say," *Christian Science Monitor,* March 24, 2006.

56. Ian Allison et al., *The Copenhagen Diagnosis,* 38.

57. See the study cited earlier (Martin Vermeer and Stefan Rahmstorf, "Global Sea Level Linked to Global Temperature.") The IPCC Fourth Assessment put the upper end estimate of seal level rise at 59 centimeters and this latest study puts the upper estimate at 190 centimeters.

58. Julian Siddle, "Marine Life Faces 'Acid Threat,'" BBC News, November 25, 2008. For the study that is being referred to see J. Timothy Wootton, Catherine A. Pfister, and James D. Forester, "Dynamic Patterns and Ecological Impacts of Declining Ocean pH in a High-Resolution Multi-Year Dataset," PNAS 105, no. 48 (December 2, 2008): 18848–53, *www.pnas.org/content/early/2008/11/24/0810079105.full.pdf+html.*

59. Stanford University, "Lower Increases in Global Temperatures Could Lead to Greater Impacts Than Previously Thought, Study Finds," *Science Daily,* March 1, 2009, *www.sciencedaily.com/releases/2009/02/090223221425.htm.*

60. John Cox, *Climate Crash: Abrupt Climate Change and What It Means for Our Future* (Washington, D.C.: National Academies Press, 2005), 189.

61. Ibid, 190.

62. James Hansen et al., "Target Atmospheric CO_2: Where Should Humanity Aim?" *Open Atmospheric Science Journal* 2 (2008): 217–31. For a less technical explanation of his argument see chapter 8 of James Hansen, *Storms of My Grandchildren: The Truth about the Coming Climate Catastrophe and Our Last Chance to Save Humanity* (New York: Bloomsbury USA, 2009). Other major scientists around the world agree with Hansen, including Hans Joachim Schellenhuber. See J. Rockstrom et al., "A Safe Operating Space for Humanity, *Nature* 461 (2009): 472–75.

63. Hansen, *Storms of My Grandchildren,* 160.

64. Ibid.

65. Ibid., 165.

66. Ibid.

67. Ibid., 160

68. Ibid., 38.

69. Ibid., 83.

70. Rob Young and Orrin Pilkey, "How High Will Seas Rise? Get Ready for Seven Feet," *Yale Environment 360* (January 14, 2010). Young and Pilkey are authors of *Rising Sea* (Washington, D.C.: Island Press, 2009).

71. Ibid.

72. Ibid.

73. Hansen et al., "Target Atmospheric CO_2: Where Should Humanity Aim?" 217.

74. See Keith Kloor, "The Eye of the Storm," *Nature Reports Climate Change,* November 26, 2009; Elizabeth Kolbert, "The Catastrophist: NASA's Climate Expert Delivers the News No One Wants to Hear," *New Yorker,* June 29, 2009, 39. Mark Bowen, *Censoring Science: Inside the Political Attack on Dr. James Hansen and the Truth of Global Warming* (New York: Plume, 2009).

75. Institute for Governance and Sustainable Development, "Tipping Points for Abrupt Climate Change: The Shadow That Haunts Climate Policy," *IGSD Climate Briefing Note,* October 5, 2008, 3, fn. 21. IPCC (2001).

76. National Academy of Sciences Committee on Abrupt Climate Change, National Research Council, *Abrupt Climate Change: Inevitable Surprises* (Washington, D.C.: National Academies Press, 2001), 1.

77. Fred Pearce, *With Speed and Violence: Why Scientists Fear Tipping Points in Climate Change* (Boston: Beacon Press, 2007), 23.

78. Andrew C. Revkin, " 'Tipping Points' and the Climate Challenge," *New York Times,* March 28, 2009.

79. Wallace S. Broecker, "Unpleasant Surprises in the Greenhouse?" *Nature* 328 (July 9, 1987): 123–26 at 126. Although climate models have improved greatly over the twenty years since Broecker wrote this article, Broecker's concern has "been confirmed repeatedly, in studies that Broecker has devoted much of his time to analyzing and catalyzing: climate is not stable. On the contrary, it is a tetchy beast, subject to large and abrupt mood swings." Wallace S. Broecker and Robert Kunzig, *Fixing Climate: What Past Climate Changes Reveal about the Current Threat — and How to Counter It* (New York: Hill and Wang, 2008), xii.

80. Broecker, "Unpleasant Surprises in the Greenhouse?" 123.

81. National Academy of Sciences, *Abrupt Climate Change,* 107.

82. Deborah Zabarenko, "Human Warming Hobbles Ancient Climate Cycle," *Reuters,* April 27, 2008. This piece in Reuters is referencing the following paper: Richard E. Zeebe and Ken Caldeira, "Close Mass Balance of Long-Term Carbon Fluxes from Ice-Core CO_2 and Ocean Chemistry Records," *Nature Geoscience* 1 (2008): 312–15.

83. See Hans Joachim Schellenhuber, "The MAD Challenge: Towards a Great Land-Use Transformation?" Plenary Session of International Scientific Congress — Climate Change: Global Risks, Challenges & Decisions — March 12, 2009. His presentation can be viewed at *http://climatecongress.ku.dk/webcasts/*.

84. Dean, "Emissions Cut Won't Bring Quick Relief, Scientists Say."

85. Fred Pearce, "Consumption Dwarfs Population as Main Environmental Threat," *Yale Environment 360* (April 13, 2009), *http://e360.yale.edu/content/feature.msp?id=2140*. Pearce's figures come from Stephen Pacala, who is director of the Princeton Environment Institute.

86. Hansen, *Storms of My Grandchildren,* 189.

87. Ibid.

88. U.S. Department of Energy, "Report to Congress on Assessment of Potential Impact of Concentrating Solar Power for Electricity Generation (EPACT 2005 — Section 934 (c))," (February 2007), 7.

89. Joseph Romm, "The Technology That Will Save Humanity," *Salon.com,* April 14, 2008, 3.

90. Ibid., 1, 3.

91. Ibid., 3.

92. Ibid., 3.

93. Lester Brown, *Plan B 3.0,* 252.

94. Ibid., 239.

95. Ibid.

96. Ibid., The study Brown is citing is Cristina L. Archer and Mark Z. Jacobson, "Evaluation of Global Windpower," *Journal of Geophysical Research* 110 (June 30, 2005).

97. Lester Brown, *Plan B 3.0,* 239.

98. Louis Bergeron, "Study: Shifting the World to 100 percent Clean, Renewable Energy by 2030 — Here Are the Numbers," Stanford Report, October 20, 2009, *http://news.stanford.edu/news/2009/october19/ jacobson-energy-study-102009.html*. See also a synopsis of the study: Mark Z. Jacobson and Mark Delucchi, "A Path to Sustainable Energy by 2030," *Scientific American* (November 2009).

99. Jon Creyts, Anton Derkach, Scott Nyquist, Ken Ostrowski, and Jack Stephenson, "Reducing U.S. Greenhouse Gas Emissions: *How*

Much at What Cost?" McKinsey & Company (December 2007). See *www.mckinsey.com/clientservice/ccsi/pdf/US_ghg_final_report.pdf.*

100. Edmund L. Andrews and Peter Baker, "A.I.G. Planning Huge Bonuses after $170 Billion Bailout," *New York Times,* March 14, 2009.

101. Liz Halloran, "Outrage Over AIG Politically Tricky for Obama," *NPR,* March 16, 2009. Jackie Calmes and Louise Story, "Outcry Builds in Washington for Recovery of A.I.G. Bonuses," *New York Times,* March 17, 2009; Brady Dennis and David Cho, "Rage at AIG Swells as Bonuses Go Out," *Washington Post,* March 17, 2009.

102. Carl Hulse and David M. Herszenhorn, "House Approves 90 Percent Tax on Bonuses after Bailouts," *New York Times,* March 19, 2009.

103. Deborah Solomon, "Questions for Steven Chu: The Science Guy," *New York Times,* April 16, 2009.

104. Alison Benjamin, "Stern: Climate Change a 'Market Failure,' " *The Guardian,* November 29, 2007.

105. Authors of Copenhagen Diagnosis, "Emissions Cut of 40 percent below 1990 Levels by 2020 Needed for Industrial Countries for 2 degree C Limit," International Media Releases and Press Conferences, December 15, 2009, *www.copenhagendiagnosis.org/press.html.*

106. See ibid. and German Advisory Council on Global Change, "Climate Change: Why 2 degrees C?" Factsheet no. 2 (2009), *www.wbgu.de/ wbgu_factsheet_2_en.pdf.*

107. *http://catholicclimatecovenant.org/.*

108. *www.catholicsandclimatechange.org/.*

109. *www.earth-policy.org/.*

110. *www.earth-policy.org/index.php?/books/pb4/pb4_presentation.*

111. *www.wecansolveit.org.*

112. It is important that letters sent to Congress are not form letters from a particular organization, but personal letters. See the results of the survey of congressional staff members: *Communicating with Congress: How Capital Hill Is Coping with the Surge in Citizen Advocacy* (Washington, D.C.: Congressional Management Foundation, 2005), 30–31.

113. SourceWatch, "What Happened to the 151 Proposed Coal Plants?" Center for Media and Democracy, *www.sourcewatch.org/index.php?title= What_happened_to_the_151_proposed_coal_plants%3F* (accessed January 10, 2010); Sierra Club, "Stopping Coal in Its Tracks" at *www.sierraclub.org/environmentallaw/coal/plantlist.asp* and the Sierra Club beyond Coal Campaign at *www.sierraclub.org/Coal/.*

114. The 3.5 degree Celsius assessment comes from Climate Action Tracker, which is affiliated with major scientific centers, including the Potsdam Institute for Climate Impacts Research. It can be accessed at

www.climateactiontracker.org/. The 3.9 degree assessment comes from Climate Interactive, affiliated with the Sustainability Institute, Ventana Systems, and the Massachusetts Institute of Technology. It can be accessed at *http://climateinteractive.org/scoreboard/scoreboard-science-and-data/ climate-interactive-scoreboard.*

115. Pope Benedict XVI, "If You Want to Cultivate Peace, Protect Creation," Message for the Celebration of the World Day of Peace (January 1, 2010), par. 4.

TWO

The Bible's Wisdom Tradition and Creation Theology

Dianne Bergant, C.S.A.

TRADITIONALLY THE WORLDVIEW of Christian believers has been shaped by a form of anthropocentrism, a view that places the human person at the center of perception and the measure according to which everything else is to be evaluated. A great deal of what has been called modern progress owes its existence and development to this perspective. However, critics, prominent among them Lynn White,[1] blame such an anthropocentric viewpoint, or an exaggeration of it, for much of the turmoil in contemporary society as well as for the current and pressing global environmental crises. On the other hand, the supporters of such a perspective assert that an anthropocentric bias can be validated by the biblical tradition, specifically the Genesis 1 creation narrative where the first man and woman are given the commission to subdue the earth and have dominion over the rest of creation. According to this view, humankind was not only the culmination of creation but also its goal. It is easy to understand how human beings imbued with such a worldview and biblical understanding might exploit the natural world in order to accomplish their own goals.

In the face of this, we must ask several crucial questions: Is it possible that the Bible is not as anthropocentric as we have presumed? Could it be that a text's apparent anthropocentric emphasis simply marks the limitations of a particular historical culture? Might it really be intended to serve a theological or social goal rather than describe the reality of humankind's place within the broader creation? For example, might the apparent hostility toward the forces

35

of nature, as described in many of the prophetic texts, actually be an Israelite polemic against nature deities that might have been thought to rival the sovereignty of YHWH? Or is it possible that what appears to be an anthropocentric bias might instead be an ethnocentric defense of Israel's monotheistic perspective?

People of the biblical eras, like most traditional societies, had a point of view that was much more holistic than ours. Because they were more directly dependent upon the natural world, they quite easily espoused aspects of harmony and interdependence within all creation that often escape us. They may not have been biocentric or cosmocentric — points of view toward which many people are moving today — but they were certainly theocentric or God-centered. The lives of the people were directed by their understanding of some divine plan or goal unfolding within the world.

On the other hand, might an anthropocentric point of view have been imposed by the biblical reader rather than implied by the biblical author? Much of the interpretation that shaped the way we understand the Bible today took shape during the nineteenth century. The scientific discoveries of the sixteenth and seventeenth centuries greatly influenced Western culture's view of human ability and excellence. During those centuries, several great minds first began to understand the physical forces at work in the universe. As scientists invented new technologies that could manipulate and control the environment for human advantage, a very significant theological shift began to take place. The eschatological expectation of fulfillment was thought to be on the horizon, and its achievement seemed to be within the power and reach of human beings. God may have been the original creator, but it seemed that human genius could now bring forth the "new creation." Progress took on a quasi-divine appearance, and this was exaggerated by the undeniable good that it produced. Human life was enriched, human dignity was enhanced, and human beings seemed to hold their destiny in their own hands. Exaggerated anthropocentrism was in its glory. Everything was judged from the perspective of its value to human progress. Most likely, this point of view was read into many biblical texts.

Today new methods of interpretation provide innovative, even subversive, readings of many biblical passages (various forms of liberationist, cultural exegesis, postcolonialism, space theory, etc.[2]).

These methods invite us to look at biblical passages through various lenses. However, if we are able to put aside our own anthropocentric bias, a careful reading will show that extraordinary biblical methods may not always be necessary for reading the Bible in new ways. Such reading will show that the Bible itself may not be as anthropocentric as we have presumed. Our analysis of sections of two books from the Old Testament will demonstrate this.

Creation Theology in the Wisdom Tradition

The affinity of creation theology to the wisdom tradition of Israel has long been recognized. However, in such study creation regularly has been considered one theme among many, and usually one of secondary importance as compared with more familiar themes such as salvation history or prophetic critique. Wisdom theology has seldom, if ever, been considered the basis of theology. Furthermore, when descriptions of creation are not dismissed as mythological accounts of primeval origins as found in the creation traditions, creation is typically considered a feature of literary expression or nature poetry, as imagery that characterizes something other than nature itself, such as found in the Song of Songs. This is not the point of view proposed in this study. Instead, the lens through which I will examine biblical passages and the standard against which these passages will be evaluated will be a perspective sensitive to the integrity of creation, not one flowing from the bias and tyranny of unyielding anthropocentrism, which has held sway for so long.

Job

Who does not know the story found in the book of Job? Most people are familiar only with the folktale (chapters 1 and 2 and the last ten verses of chapter 42) that frames the major part of the book. This folktale tells of a righteous man who suffered great calamities. Despite his unexplained plight, he clung to his righteousness, and God rewarded him for his fidelity. This abbreviated knowledge of the book misses the description of Job's real struggle with his perception of God's insensitivity, even injustice, toward him. It also fails to see how Job is transformed by his experience of God.

It is in the poetic section of the book that we discover that it was only after long and apparently pointless arguments with his unsympathetic visitors that Job turns to God and demands some kind of explanation for the suffering that has inexplicably overwhelmed him. God does respond, but with questions rather than answers, and the questions address the design and operation of the natural world and not the specifics of Job's afflictions. That God would ask questions and that these questions directed Job's attention to the workings of the natural world is in keeping with the character of wisdom thinking. First, in this book, God is portrayed as leading Job from one way of perceiving reality to another. In other words, God is a teacher, and asking questions in order to accomplish this is a well-established pedagogical technique. Furthermore, using aspects of the natural world to uncover dimensions of the world of human beings is also a well-known method of wisdom teaching. Sayings such as "Go to the ant, O sluggard" (Prov 6:6), and stories about animals as found in Aesop's tales are evidence of this approach.

As we marvel at the vistas of creation painted by God's investigation of Job, the distinctive form of the questions that God poses should not be overlooked. These are not requests for information. They are ironic questions that serve to correct Job's shortsighted perception of his ability to grasp the mysteries of life in general and his own life in particular. "Where were you when I founded the earth? ... Have you ever in your lifetime commanded the morning and shown the dawn its place? ... Do you know about the birth of the mountain goats? ... Do you give the horse his strength, and endow his neck with splendor?" (Job 38:4, 12; 39:1, 19). These are rhetorical questions[3] meant to lead Job to a depth of understanding far greater than any level of knowledge mere answers would provide. The marvel of this questioning technique is seen in its ability to bring Job to real wisdom despite, or perhaps because of, the indirectness of the approach. God asks questions about cosmic nature and Job gains insight into human nature.

Perhaps the most neglected characteristic of this multifaceted biblical book is the revelatory significance of nature depicted within it. Nature is not the principal marvel that is showcased here. Rather, it is the awesome God who is manifested through the natural world. In other words, the artistry of God can be seen in the splendor of the universe; God's wisdom in its delicate balance; God's imagination in its diversity; God's providence in its inherent fruitfulness. The natural world was not only born of the creativity of God; it also bears the features of this creativity. Every property of creation mirrors something of the creator. It is not enough to say that creation is the medium through which God is revealed. In a very real sense, the medium is itself the revelation. Job states this in his final response ("now my eyes have seen you," Job 42:5). There he testifies to having seen something of God, not merely of the splendor of creation.

The wonders of creation that are paraded before Job were not unknown to him before this extraordinary revelation. By and large, they constituted the everyday world that he knew, but which he did not understand; the ordinary world within which he lived, but which he seems to have taken for granted. This breathtaking, even mystical, experience of creation has catapulted Job out of the narrow confines of his finite anthropocentrism into the vast expanses of mystery. It has brought him to realize that human history unfolds within the broader context of the natural world, and not the natural world within the parameters of human history. Job comes to see that the natural world does not merely serve the ends of human history. His encounter with the ineffable creator-God has led him to this new insight. It is an insight that transforms him from a self-pitying victim of circumstances to a human being who has endured the struggles of human finitude and emerged chastened, yet nonetheless a mystic.

In his last response to God, Job admits that he has been converted to God's point of view, even without comprehending it. Job's previous understanding characterized God as a God of righteousness, one who had recognized Job's integrity and apparently had rewarded him for it. Job's new understanding conceived of a mysterious power that brought forth the world, as a man begets or as a woman gives birth, a God who is somehow revealed in and through that wondrous world. This is a God who can provide for the entire resplendent universe without being distracted from the specific needs of fragile human beings. God can do this, because God's designs are grander than, yet still include, human history.

God has taken human suffering, the most pressing concern of human life, and has situated it within a broader context. That context is material creation in its entirety. The YHWH speeches have shown Job that, in the midst of measureless natural grandeur, the ambiguity of human life can be confronted with the honesty and humility that it requires, an honesty and humility that can admit to and accept the limited capacity of human comprehension. Creation itself has expanded Job's vision and called him to a deepening of faith that goes beyond understanding.

The book of Job demonstrates the profound human struggle between anthropology and cosmology, between human-centered interests and cosmocentric realities. It pits the search for understanding against the enormity of the universe in such a way that the human spirit is enraptured and not broken. The commonplace yet strangely unfamiliar natural world awakens amazement at its wonders and leaves the humbled gazer aghast. Having called on God to put things right in his particular life, Job was led by the magnitude of creation beyond himself, there to see that he could not fathom the laws by which God governs. In the end, cosmology does not defeat anthropology; rather cosmology opens its arms to welcome back anthropology, its prodigal child.

The implications of such a transformed attitude are profound as well as wide-reaching. The shift from an anthropocentric to a cosmocentric worldview requires not only a new way of understanding the universe itself, but also a reexamination of many, if not most, of the tenets of faith and the moral life. Notions such as frugality and sufficiency in our use of natural resources, the viability of human life and the earth's ability to sustain it will all play indispensable roles in theological thinking. The irresponsibility and impertinence of human self-centeredness will be replaced by a sense of respect and responsible stewardship, and the bottom line of monetary calculation of resources will give way to aesthetic contemplation of natural beauty, a contemplation not unlike that of Job who cried out in awe: "I had heard of you by word of mouth, but now my eye has seen you" (42:5).

The Wisdom of Solomon

The Wisdom of Solomon gets its name by inference. The author does not explicitly identify himself as Solomon, but, speaking in the first person, he describes himself as such (7:5; 8:21; 9:7f; cf. 1 Kings 3:5–15). However, there is ample evidence to indicate that this book originated during the Hellenistic period, hundreds of years after the time of the Israelite king. For this reason, commentators refer to the author as Pseudo-Solomon.

The book is known for its midrashic approach, a method of Jewish interpretation that takes a biblical tradition that originated in one historical situation and makes it relevant in a new one.[4] This kind of interpretation allows aspects of the biblical tradition to give faithful direction to a new generation in an entirely new context. In developing this form of reinterpretation of the exodus story, Pseudo-Solomon employs a Hellenistic form of comparison or contrast known as syncrisis.

The author of the book does not view the exodus as a military feat as is found in the book of Exodus, but as a refashioning of nature. The very sequence of events in his description follows the pattern of the creation narrative rather than the account of the liberation of the people. Here we can see how the book of Wisdom makes a unique contribution to biblical creation theology. Instead of moving from salvation to creation, as traditional Old Testament theology claims is the fundamental focus of the Bible, it begins with creation and moves to salvation. In fact, the book itself begins and ends with affirmations of God's creative purpose: "[God] created all things so that they might exist" (1:14); "The whole creation in its nature was fashioned anew...so that your children might be kept unharmed" (19:6).

In the Ancient Near Eastern view, when chaos threatens to consume the underpinnings of equanimity, the sovereign ruler of the universe has to step in and reestablish order. In the biblical tradition, this new state of accord is frequently characterized as a new creation (e.g., new heavens and new earth, Isa. 65:17; 66:22; 2 Pet. 3:13; Rev. 21:1 new spirit, Ezek. 11:19; 18:31; 36:26; new creation, 2 Cor. 5:17; Gal. 6:15; new nature, Eph. 4:24; Col. 3:10). Pseudo-Solomon seems to believe that the only way the social disorder of his time can be corrected is by means of a kind of new creation. Interpreting the miracle accounts found in the book of Exodus, he shows that nature has more than mere instrumental value; it works according to its own laws to create a new world. Although the ancient worldview was prescientific, in its own way it did respect the intrinsic value of the world and all of its components, and it did recognize the interconnectedness of all of these components.

The midrashic reflection on certain events recorded in the book of Exodus found in the third section of the Wisdom of Solomon (11:2–19:22) shows how Wisdom actually directed the course of history. The section consists of several syncrises,[5] contrasts that compare the plight of the Israelites with that of the Egyptians (scholars are not in agreement as to the exact number of syncrises.[6]) The contrasts themselves function in several ways. Most obviously, they demonstrate the theory of retribution: the righteous are rewarded while the wicked are punished. A closer look shows that natural occurrences are active in Israel's blessing as well as in Egypt's chastisement ("For by the things through which their foes were punished, they in their need were benefited," 11:5).

Various syncrises compare the way the Egyptians were plagued by the water of the Nile turned into blood, while the Israelites benefited from water that sprang from the rock; the way the Egyptians, who engaged in animal-form worship, were plagued by certain small animals, while the Israelites were fed by other small creatures (16:1f); the way the heavens poured down both water and fire, which consumed the fruits of the land of Egypt, while the same heavens rained manna, which sustained the Israelites in their need; the plague of darkness that befell the Egyptians with the pillar of light that led the Israelites to safety; and finally the decision of the Egyptians to massacre the sons of the Hebrews reverted onto their own sons.

It should be noted that these events were not perceived as miraculous interventions by God, as was the case with the earlier version of the plagues found in the book of Exodus (chapters 7–11). Rather, the text clearly states that nature, following definite natural laws (19:6–13), protected and provided for God's people as if reward and punishment were built right into the structures of the universe ("For all creation, in its several kinds, was being made anew, serving its natural laws, that your children might be preserved unharmed" — Wis. 11:6).

Even a cursory examination of these syncrises reveals the distinctiveness of Pseudo-Solomon's creation theology. Each of the syncrises attests to divine involvement. (1) In the wilderness the thirst of the Israelites was slaked, because God "gave them abundant water unexpectedly" (11:7). (2) God "tested them as a parent does," but "examined the ungodly as a stern king does" (11:10).

Furthermore, God "sent a multitude of irrational creatures to punish" the wicked (11:15), but for the Israelites God "prepared quails to eat" (16:2). (3) The ungodly "were flogged by the strength of your hand" (16:16), while "you gave your people food of angels" (16:20). (4) While lawless people languished in darkness, "You provided a flaming pillar of fire as a guide for your people's unknown journey" (18:3). (5) The greatest blow occurred when God "in punishment took away a multitude of their [Egyptian] children" (18:5), "for by the same means by which you punished our enemies you called us to yourself and glorified us" (18:8).

At first glance, this would indicate that God affects the respective suffering or blessing through the agency of creation. This suggests that creation's value is seen in its usefulness. In other words, its value is instrumental. However, at other times it appears that the universe itself is on the side of righteousness. This suggests a kind of intrinsic value, a value that is inherent in creation itself. Even more striking is the claim that, when creation does take sides with the just, it is actually working according to certain natural laws, "serving its own laws" (19:6), not because of any divine intervention. This is a bold claim, because in these instances, especially the event of the crossing of the sea, nature acts in a way that seems to be outside the boundaries of its laws. How can it be complying with laws in these instances? In addressing this situation, Pseudo-Solomon claims that "all of creation, in its several kinds, [is] being made over anew" (19:6) and now " . . . serving you its maker, grows tense for punishment against the wicked but is relaxed in benefit for those who trust you" (16:24). According to Pseudo-Solomon, creation is indeed working in accord with natural laws, but in a transformed manner.

Such a claim about the transformation of nature is made from within Pseudo-Solomon's philosophical understanding of the Greek principle of mutual interchangeability[7] ("For the elements, in variable harmony among themselves, like strings of a harp, produce new melody, while the flow of music steadily persists," 19:18). According to this Stoic doctrine, the basic material substance of a thing remains the same. However, periodically there occurs an interchange of the elements of which it is composed. This results in an alteration in its individual combinations without a fundamental change in its substance. Thus, having been, in some sense, created anew, nature can still follow its own laws and yet act in astonishing new ways. Pseudo-Solomon uses musical notes to exemplify what he means. A musician can produce several different tunes using the same musical notes in different combinations. Using this metaphor, he explains how the harmony within creation was not disturbed by these remarkable occurrences. Rather, a different harmony was simply produced.

The principle of mutual interchangeability may provide an explanation of how the events described could have occurred, but it does not explain why they happened. Was it a chance exchange of elements? Or did something in nature itself trigger the process of interchange? If the latter was the case, that is, if something in nature triggered the interchange, what might it have been? On the other hand, did God direct the transformation? If this was the situation, what was God's reason for doing so? It is clear from the biblical text itself that this was no chance exchange of elements. Nor was it exclusively an event of nature. Therefore, the first two suggested explanations must be rejected.

The syncrises plainly state that God is the one who directed the exceptional natural phenomena. But why? From an ethnocentric point of view, one could say that the change occurred because of God's bias in favor of the Israelites. They were afflicted, and so God intervened on their behalf. From a theological point of view, one could say that it happened because of God's passion for justice. The wicked had been prospering and the upright had been suffering, and so God reversed their fates: the wicked were now punished and the just rewarded. While each of these explanations is in some way quite valid, the solutions that they propose require only a suspension of the natural laws, as the original account in the book of Exodus seems to describe. They do not tell us why, as this account clearly states, creation was refashioned.

Two very different concepts come together here to answer this question. One is the concept of theodicy: the defense of the justice of God in the face of injustice. The other is the principle of mutual interchangeability. Theodicy is really the pressing concern here. It presumes two fundamental concepts. First, there is an underlying order upon which reality, at least moral human reality, is based. Second, this order is auspicious and the God who created it and who oversees it is trustworthy. Many traditional societies believed that there is a direct connection between the laws that govern the cosmos and those that are operative in human society. They held that a change in one sphere has repercussions in the other. From this they concluded that any dissension among the gods significantly affects human society; any disruption in human social harmony endangers the order of the universe.

A worldview that presumes such fundamental interdependence most likely can deal with the kinds of change that come with living, but it can hardly endure significant upheaval. In this view, when chaos does threaten to consume the underpinnings of equanimity, the sovereign ruler of the universe has to step in and reestablish order. Pseudo-Solomon clearly envisions such an interdependent universe, and he seems to believe that the only way the social disorder can be corrected is by means of a kind of new creation. Given the philosophical worldview of his time, the doctrine of mutual interchangeability explains the way this might happen.

Using this doctrine to reinterpret the miracle accounts found in the book of Exodus, Pseudo-Solomon shows that nature has more than mere instrumental value; it works according to its own laws. Although the ancient worldview was pre-scientific, in its own way it did respect the intrinsic value of the world and all of its components, and it did recognize the interconnectedness of all of these components.

Ancient Biblical Theology as Contemporary Ecotheology

Can the message of these biblical books be revelatory for us today, or is the worldview that produced them so scientifically naive that new eco-sensitive readings are unfeasible? It is very difficult to critique one worldview according to the principles of another. However, if we are to open ourselves to the revelatory possibilities of the biblical tradition without being captive to its limitations, we are obliged to do just that. We must also be attentive to the biases that color both our worldview and the approaches that we employ in our examination. As we grow in sensitivity to ecological issues, we might detect in the biblical writings what appears to us to be a disregard of the intrinsic value of the created world. We must never forget that we are able to recognize these attitudes because we have gained insight shaped by scientific inquiry, with eyes that tend to compartmentalize reality. Without trying to assume an ancient worldview with its perspectives and principles, we certainly can attempt to enflesh some of its theological insights into our own religious imagination.

Although most people think that the primary focus of the book of Job is the question of innocent suffering, a careful reading of the speeches of God shows that Job's suffering was merely the occasion for a radical shift in his point of view. His suffering certainly caused him great distress, but even more so did his inability to understand why he was suffering. And what did he learn from God's questioning? That God is not only in charge of the wonders of creation, but that those wonders are held within the balance and harmony of divine providence. Furthermore, human beings are unable to grasp the scope of this providence. Job had to readjust his view of human capability.

In the age in which we live, an age of great accomplishment and promise, we would do well to consider the lesson about the limitations of human nature that Job learned. It is a lesson that seems learned only the hard way, through failure or suffering, for we really only discover our limits when we are up against them. Still, many today not only fail to recognize human limits, but they do not even seem to be conscious of the fact that we have limits. Contemporary slogans are telling. They claim: "You can do anything you put your mind to," or "the sky's the limit." Perhaps we should think more along the lines of Job's thought: "I have dealt with great things I do not understand; things too wonderful for me, which I cannot know. . . . I disown what I have said, and repent in dust and ashes" (Job 42:3, 6).

The book of Wisdom teaches the interdependence of all elements of creation. Its pre-scientific understanding of this harmony may well have been somewhat naïve, but new science insists that all elements of creation are indeed interdependent. We are a part of this world, made of it, and dependent on it for our survival. Previous scientific and religious understanding led us to separate ourselves from the rest of the natural world, to assume to ourselves an attitude of supremacy, and to look with disdain on what is not human. This disdain gave rise to many of the ecological ills from which Earth suffers today.

We are often so accustomed to using the things of Earth for our own purposes that we may fail to think of what we are doing to it.

Nature itself has devised a mysterious and delicate balance whereby it continually renews itself. Death in one form gives way to life in a new form. Both animate and inanimate creatures are governed by patterns of development that have brought forth the wondrous world of nature as we know it. These dynamic patterns regularly refashion the earth. However, if we intrude into the workings of nature without replacing what we have taken or leave behind only the debris of our manipulation, we throw into jeopardy the balance of the environment that is essential for our survival.

We alone of all the creatures of the earth can take hold of the powers of creation and reshape them for our own advancement. We alone have discovered fire and harnessed the energies of water, the wind, the sun, and the atom. We alone have the future Earth's well-being and survival in our hands. Possessing such power, we must never forget that we are only a part of this mysterious ecosystem. We must cherish Earth, nurture its fruitfulness and foster its growth. We must live in accord with our world or we will not live at all. We must walk through our world with dignity and responsibility, with understanding and trustworthiness. It is an awesome role that we play in the world. It makes us stand in wonder at the magnificence of this universe and at the dignity with which God has clothed us.

When we live in harmony with the rest of the natural world we will be drawn into the secrets of its heart, there to find God. We will be sensitive to its twists and turns, to its cries and to its silences, and know God's presence through it all. We will learn what it has to teach us of the creative amusement of God, of the youthful imagination of God, of the profound wisdom of God. Biblical characters like Job and Pseudo-Solomon point the way for us to look on the face of God, as revealed through the natural world, and live.

Notes

1. Lynn White, "The Religious Roots of Our Ecological Crisis," *Science* (1967), 1203–7.

2. Elisabeth Schüssler Fiorenza, ed., *Searching the Scriptures: A Feminist Commentary* (New York: Crossroad, 1994); Norman K. Gottwald and Richard A. Horsley, eds., *The Bible and Liberation: Political and Social Hermeneutics,* rev. ed. (Maryknoll, N.Y.: Orbis Books, 1993); Fernando F. Segovia and Mary Ann Tolbert, eds., *Reading*

from This Place: Social Location and Biblical Interpretation in Global Perspective (Minneapolis: Fortress Press, 1995); Stephen D. Moore and Fernando F. Segovia, eds., *Postcolonial Biblical Criticism: Interdisciplinary Intersections* (New York: T & T Clark, 2005); A. K. M. Adam, ed., *Handbook of Postmodern Biblical Interpretation* (St. Louis: Chalice Press, 2000).

3. Norman C. Habel, *The Book of Job,* Old Testament Library (Philadelphia: Westminster Press, 1985); John E. Hartley, *The Book of Job,* the New International Commentary on the Old Testament (Grand Rapids: Eerdmans, 1988), 487–89; Gerald H. Wilson, *Job,* New International Biblical Commentary (Peabody, Mass.: Hendrickson Publishers, 2007), 420–21.

4. James M. Reese, *Hellenistic Influence on the Book of Wisdom and Its Consequences* (Rome: Biblical Institute Press, 1970), 91–102; Peter Enns, *Exodus Retold: Ancient Exegesis of the Departure from Egypt in Wis 10:15–21 and 19:1–9,* Harvard Semitic Museum Monographs 57 (1997), 15–17; for an opposing view see Samuel Cheon, "The Exodus Story in the Wisdom of Solomon: A Study in Biblical Interpretation," *Journal for the Study of the Pseudepigrapha,* Supplement Series 23 (Sheffield, UK: Sheffield Press,1997) 13f.

5. For an explanation of syncrisis see David Winston, *The Wisdom of Solomon,* Anchor Bible (New York: Doubleday, 1979), 227–28.

6. Some scholars believe that there are five syncrises: Roland E. Murphy, *The Tree of Life,* Anchor Bible Reference Library (New York: Doubleday, 1990), 90–91; Leo G. Perdue, *Wisdom and Creation: The Theology of Wisdom Literature* (Nashville: Abingdon Press, 1994), 294; Addison G. Wright, "The Structure of the Book of Wisdom," in *Biblica* (1967): 117. Others maintain that there are seven: Reese, *Hellenistic Influence on the Book of Wisdom and Its Consequences,* 98–102; Winston, *The Wisdom of Solomon,* 227; Cheon, "The Exodus Story in the Wisdom of Solomon," 25.

7. Sometimes referred to as universal intermingling, Marcia L. Colish, *The Stoic Tradition from Antiquity to the Early Middle Ages* (Leiden: E. J. Brill, 1985), 25. See also David Winston, "The Book of Wisdom's Theory of Cosmology," in *History of Religions* 11 (1971): 195; Cheon, "The Exodus Story in the Wisdom of Solomon," 104–5; Philo, *De Vito Mosis* 2:48, 266–67.

THREE

Creation, Incarnation, and Resurrection

John J. O'Keefe

SOME IDEAS REALLY STICK. Growing up in the 1960s and '70s I was a huge fan of the television series *Star Trek*. My enthusiasm was renewed in the 1980s with the arrival of *Star Trek: The Next Generation* and the other series and feature films that bear that brand — *Deep Space 9*, and *Voyager*, to name two of these. The second wave of *Star Trek* corresponded with the beginning of my own theological education. Although I do not recall exactly when, at some point I began to notice that whenever *Star Trek* did an episode that depicted the evolution of an intelligent life form it always did so by suggesting a movement from matter toward spirit.

For example, in the *Star Trek: The Next Generation* episode *Transfigurations*, which aired in 1990, the *Enterprise* encounters a wounded alien with amnesia. As the alien, named "John Doe" by the crew, begins to recover, the ship's doctor discovers both that the alien has unusual healing powers and that his body is undergoing rapid genetic mutation. Meanwhile, some other members of the alien race, now called the Zalkonians, catch up with the *Enterprise* and demand the return of John, who they say is a "mutant" criminal. As the plot unfolds, the viewer discovers that the entire race of Zalkonians is on the verge of evolving into a new form of life. "John" and a few others like him represent the leading edge of this transformation and are being persecuted because of what they represent to those who have not yet begun to change. At the end of the episode, "John" gives himself over to the process of mutation

49

and is transformed into pure energy. Free from the constraints of his body, he disappears through the ship's hull into deep space.

On the one hand, the idea that this *Star Trek* story suggests is merely the stuff of science fiction. Yet, on the other hand, it presents a view of human nature and human destiny that runs deep in our cultural imagination, which, I would argue, has roots in Christian discourse.[1] For centuries, the traditions of Christian spirituality have suggested that the trajectory of salvation begins in body and ends in spirit. Most Christians, in my experience, do not hold the words "material" and "spiritual" together when thinking about postmortem existence. My students, who are typical representatives of our culture, when asked to describe their own images of the afterlife inevitably say things like "it is very white and bright." They think of clouds and other things thin and lofty. They rarely think of life with God as being in some way continuous with this life: a renewed existence in a material context. So when the writers of *Star Trek* wished to depict the evolution of Zalkonians, they instinctively depicted this as a movement from matter toward spirit or, to speak more scientifically, as a movement from matter toward energy.

As those of you who are familiar with the intellectual side of the environmental movement know, it is precisely here that many non-Christian environmental writers offer significant critiques of Christianity. In their view, if we imagine ourselves as fundamentally spirits awaiting liberation from our bodies, we introduce the possibility of thinking of ourselves as something other than nature. The Christian idea of evolution toward spirit, again in this view, makes it possible for humans to adopt exploitative attitudes toward the natural world because they think of themselves as, deep down, really belonging to another dimension of reality and because they see this world and this life as something they need to get through. Many of these non-Christian authors, if they have a religious imagination, tend to lean toward a mystical pantheism and imagine their lives as emerging from and returning to the rich fecundity of the material universe.[2]

As an example of this way of thinking, permit me to offer one more example from the world of fiction. In his celebrated series *His Dark Materials*, author Philip Pullman writes with some passion about the potential redemptive power of this pantheist vision. The three books in the series, *The Golden Compass, The Subtle Knife,* and *The Amber Spyglass,* are beautifully written and completely engaging stories. They are also profoundly lyrical and romantic. Although written for children, they are not just books for children, but offer an imaginative retelling of Milton's *Paradise Lost,* in which human beings rebelling against the limits of their own nature nearly destroy all reality.[3] Yet Pullman is no Christian: his religious vision, if there is one, is wrapped up in his deep love for the universe and its profound physicality.

The fantasy world that Pullman creates is complex, but one detail is essential for the point I wish to make here. Throughout the novels human beings carry around with them at all times an external personification of their souls called a daemon. These daemons take an animal form that is appropriate to the character of their humans. Daemons also vanish and dissipate immediately upon the death of their human. Thus, unlike the Christian idea of the soul as invisible but immortal, Pullman's daemons are visible but mortal. In one particular scene the main characters, Lyra and Will, travel to the land of the dead in an effort to free the dead from a wraithlike existence far from light and embodiment. The dead have been imprisoned there by an evil force. Without their daemon-souls, their lives are a shadowy misery of despair and grief. As the story unfolds, however, the reader understands that for these imprisoned shadows freedom from the land of the dead will not result in a renewed spiritual existence with God: instead, the dead will be released back into the dust from which they came and be recycled by the benevolent cosmos. Here is Lyra's speech to the dead just before their liberation from their underworld prison:

> "This is what'll happen," she said, "and it's true, perfectly true. When you go out of here, all the particles that make you up will loosen and float apart, just like your daemons did. If you've seen people dying, you know what that looks like. But your daemons aren't just nothing now; they're part of everything. All the atoms that were them, they've gone into the air and the wind and the trees and the earth and all the living things. They'll never vanish. They're just part of everything. And that's exactly what'll happen to you, I swear to you, I promise on my honor. You'll drift apart, it's true, but you'll be out in the open, part of everything alive again."[4]

When the dead emerge from the underworld, one by one the remnants of their material forms dissolve and, in a final ecstatic moment, they are released from their particular identities into the universal all. Although Pullman's description of the ecstatic reintegration of the dead with the cosmos is clearly not Christian, it is not unattractive, at least in the way he narrates it. Indeed, as I will discuss later, a surprising number of Christians have been attracted to this eschatology in their efforts to escape from the antimaterial implications of a *Star-Trek*-like theory of spiritual progress.

In my own reading of the spiritual side of the environmental movement, it seems that the religious imaginations of many Christians are stuck in either the paradigm exemplified by *Star Trek* or in the paradigm exemplified by the fictional characters in Philip Pullman's novels. At the same time, Christian theological reflection on the environment has been taking place, for the most part, among ethicists. While I applaud the attention given to ethics, in my view we also need to devote intellectual energy to a reexamination of our core doctrines in the light of the environmental challenges we face. Questions such as why is there a world at all? why do humans struggle in it? and what is the nature of salvation? are at least as important for fostering a truly Christian environmental consciousness as questions such as how should we live? and what should we do?

Christian environmental reasoning begins with the doctrine of creation. Or, to state this more precisely, it begins with an interpretation of the meaning of creation and the relationship of human beings to all other creatures. The prime narrative of this relationship is, of course, the creation story contained in the first chapters of Genesis. In those chapters God is said to have created the world, the world is good, and the human beings have a special place in the world. Indeed, humans have a relationship of "dominion" over God's creation (see Gen. 1:27–31). Humans are also said to be both made from dust and, at the same time, to have been made in the image and likeness of God. This story contains many possible interpretive paths to follow. Clearly one of these emerges from tracing out the meaning of the word "dominion." What, exactly, is the nature of the "dominion" that God intended to give the human race when the world was new? Answering this question has been a major concern of environmental ethics. Indeed, Catholic (and Christian) environmental ethics can be fairly described as an extended meditation on the implications of the idea of human dominion over nature. Most commonly in the English-speaking world the word "dominion" is interpreted to mean "stewardship" rather than "domination." "Stewardship," unlike "dominion," suggests custody and loving care. Although this model does not please many in the community of ethicists, it is the most common. Recent statements by the U.S. bishops, to mention but one example, are representative of this line of reasoning.[5]

Exploring the various meanings of stewardship, however, is not the only way to move from the narratives of Genesis toward environmental reflection. Early Christian theologians were interested in something else entirely. For them, there were no environmental problems, and, thus, there was no need for an environmental ethic. They tended to take the language of dominion at face value: humans were supposed to farm, domesticate animals, and hunt in order to stay alive. They were supposed to till the earth in whatever ways possible to promote human thriving. These attitudes were pervasive and utterly unproblematic. Indeed, one could argue that the word "dominion" has become an interpretive problem for the church only because of the very recent possibility that in exercising "dominion" humans now have the power to destroy the very conditions of their own existence.

Early Christian theologians saw different problems in Genesis. For some the issue was the goodness of the world: How could the world be good when there was clearly so much evil in it? Others were primarily interested in anthropology: How do we understand the human as both dust and divine image? What, exactly does the sacred author mean by saying humans are made in God's image and likeness? In emerging Christian theology, there was substantial agreement about the issue of the world's goodness and the origins of evil, but substantial disagreement about the relationship of dust to the divine image in the human person.

Early Christian theology answered the first question — that is, the nature of the goodness of the world and the origins of evil — through a protracted battle with Gnosticism. Gnosticism is a modern term that scholars use to describe a religious movement of broad appeal that flourished in the first few centuries C.E. The majority of those who study Gnosticism agree that, although it pre-dates Christianity as a religious worldview, certain elements within Christianity allowed the Gnostic impulse to grow and expand significantly. In a nutshell, Gnostics were dualists who radicalized ancient cosmology. While it may have been common since the time of Plato to think of the universe as a hierarchical chain of being that reached from unformed matter to pure being,[6] Gnostics turned this dichotomy into a battle between matter and spirit. Human beings, according to Gnostic mythology, were fundamentally imprisoned spirits. By some pre-cosmic tragedy and by the agency of malevolent forces afoot in the heavens, the spirit, which is our true self, has been placed in a body, and because of its embodiment has forgotten its true identity and its true destiny. The goal of salvation for a Gnostic was to liberate the spirit from matter so that it could return home. Knowledge about our true condition and about the forces that would keep us ignorant provided the means for escape in the same way a map offers a means of egress to anyone lost in a vast and unknown city. For Gnostics, Jesus came from above to give us the map and to chart for us a path back to our home in the heavens.

Gnosticism was appealing on many levels. It provided a plausible — to ancient readers anyway — solution to the seeming contrast between the God of the Old Testament and the God of the New. If the God of the Old Testament seemed more violent it was because, according to the Gnostics, he was more violent. He was in fact the architect of the prison of matter and quite different from the liberating father of Jesus. Thus, Gnosticism helped to solve some difficult exegetical problems. Similarly, Gnosticism offered a simple solution to the problem of evil. Evil was caused by the existence of the material world and the dark forces that controlled it. Matter, the stuff of the universe, dirt and bodies, all of these were the cause of evil. The spirits within us, however, were wholly good.

Because of the way that it understood scripture and the solution it offered to the problem of evil, Gnosticism appealed to many early Christians. Thus, the first real theological battle of the ancient church was a battle against Gnosticism. In that battle two theologians stand out: Irenaeus of Lyon and Origen. Their responses to Gnosticism, however, are quite different and have lasting consequences for the subsequent development of Christian attitudes toward nature. For those unfamiliar with these names, I offer a brief summary.

Irenaeus was a second-century theologian who died around 202 A.D. A native of Asia Minor, probably Smyrna (modern Izmir, Turkey), he migrated to the south of France where he served as bishop of Lyon until his death. He is best known for his polemical tract *Against the Heresies,* where he outlines his case against Gnosticism. Irenaeus's theology had a significant impact on the development of Trinitarian theology and classical Christology, primarily through the mediation of St. Athanasius and St. Cyril of Alexandria. Irenaeus was also a millenarian and preached a literal interpretation of the book of Revelation. This literalism limited his direct influence on the later tradition, which for the most part rejected such literal readings of scripture.[7]

Origen was born in Egypt around 185 A.D. A true genius, he became head of the catechetical school in Alexandria and remained there until problems with his bishop forced him to move up the coast to Caesarea in Palestine. Origen was a prolific writer and produced biblical commentaries, sermons, ascetical tracts, exploratory works in systematic theology, and even a rudimentary critical edition of the Bible called the Hexapla. Origen lived during a time of significant anti-Christian sentiment in the Roman Empire and died from injuries sustained under Roman torture. He was also controversial, both personally and intellectually. According to the church historian Eusebius, in an act of youthful zeal Origen castrated himself, trying to follow Christ's invitation to become a eunuch for the kingdom.[8] Many of his ideas, especially about creation and salvation, were condemned hundreds of years after his death at the Second Council of Constantinople in 553. In spite of this, Origen's influence was enormous, especially on the development of Christian spirituality: the monastic traditions of both the Eastern and the Western church owe much to the intellectual legacy of Origen.[9]

My purpose here, however, is not to offer an extended meditation on the biographies of Irenaeus and Origen. Much more narrowly, I wish to point to how their different responses to Gnosticism can be seen in the case of Origen as the ancient ancestor of the spirituality of *Star Trek* and in the case of Irenaeus as a possible alternative to the mysticism of Philip Pullman.

Origen was not a Gnostic, but neither was he a fan of embodiment. Unlike Gnostics, Origen rejected any form of dualism. Instead of interpreting Genesis as the narrative of a plot against spirits, Origen defended it as the narrative of the one God's creative activity to make a good world populated with good creatures. But at this point, Origen's world and our world diverge significantly. Many modern readers have noticed that the first chapters of Genesis contain two different creation stories. In the first, God creates humans, both male and female, in a single act of divine power. As the RSV renders it, "Then God said, 'Let us make humankind in our image, according to our likeness; and let them have dominion over the fish of the sea, and over the birds of the air, and over the cattle, and over all the wild animals of the earth, and over every creeping thing that creeps upon the earth'" (1:26). Later, in chapter 2, the story is different: "then the LORD God formed man from the dust of the ground, and breathed into his nostrils the breath of life; and the man became a living being" (2:7). A few verses later, God forms a woman from the rib of Adam and both are released into the newly created Garden of Eden.

Modern scripture scholars, of course, account for the existence of these two different creation stories by means of the documentary hypothesis, which states that the different stories are in fact artifacts of several ancient narrative traditions that were placed together by the priestly author in the final editing of the Genesis sequence. Modern interpreters tend to think historically and they resolve exegetical conundrums historically. Although ancient Christian intellectuals did not think like modern historians, they were careful readers of the Bible, and they did notice that these two stories are not the same. Many interpretive problems were resolved by applying a technique called allegory, where the literal narrative was understood as a code for some deeper meaning. Origen approached the problem philosophically. In his view, the two stories in Genesis were about two different aspects of the creation. Understood allegorically, the first story is an account of the creation of the spiritual (intelligible world), while the second is an account of the creation of the material world. In the first God speaks human nature and human souls into being; in the second, God creates a material place for subsequently embodied souls to live.

While Origen's suggestion sounds utterly preposterous to modern readers, it had broad appeal in the ancient world. What was controversial about his interpretation was not the idea that the two narratives describe the creation of spirit and matter in succession. What got Origen in trouble was the reason he gave for the need for matter. For him, God knew that humans would fall, so he created material bodies to protect them from the consequences of their rebellion. In the Platonic world, spirit and matter stood in a relationship of real to unreal. Pure spirit stood at one end and unformed matter at the other. The closer one came to spirit, the closer one came to reality. For Origen and his contemporaries, unformed matter was a kind of nothingness because of its vast ontological distance from God's self-sufficiency. For Origen, the fall was a kind of tumbling from beatitude into material density and a corresponding alienation from spirit. This sounds Gnostic, but it is not, at least not quite. Gnostics moralized Platonic metaphysics, equating spirit with goodness and matter with evil. For many Platonists, matter was not really evil, it was just less real. But Origen was not just a Platonist: he was also a Christian and he knew from the Genesis story that God proclaimed both creations to be good. For him, however, what was good about the second creation — the creation of the material world and of human embodiment — was that it prevented us, the humans, from falling all the way down the chain of being into nothingness: embodiment was a kind of safety net. With the full energy of the fall arrested by solidification, humans now had the opportunity to engage in the work of reclaiming their spiritual identity by following Christ.[10]

Many of Origen's ideas were unacceptable even to people in antiquity. Some, for example, objected to the idea that there are two creations and that embodiment was a provision for the fall. However, Origen's basic idea that the true destiny of the human was a spiritual destiny tended not to be challenged. Theologians influenced by Origen had a difficult time imagining material bodies in heaven and tended to think of salvation as something that was primarily spiritual. The tradition has always taught the idea of the resurrection of the body, but in the platonizing Christianity of Origen and those influenced by him, the resurrected bodies of the just had little in common with the bodies of flesh that we now inhabit.

The theology of Irenaeus stands in stark contrast to that of Origen. Like Origen, Irenaeus opposed the cosmic dualism of Gnosticism, but he did so in a completely different way. For Irenaeus, Christianity told a story about God's master plan. He called this plan the divine economy. According to Irenaeus, this plan originates with the creation, experiences the tragedy of the fall, receives the salvation of Christ, and will be manifest in its totality at the end of the world with the unveiling of a new heaven and a new earth. Irenaeus's vision is viscerally material. When God created the world he did not, as with Origen, create a spirit world and only later, as an afterthought, the material world. God created the material world we now see as part of the original plan. When human beings sinned in the Garden of Eden, they essentially broke their relationship with creation and introduced death and decay into human life. Irenaeus and many Christians of his generation were fascinated with 1 Corinthians 15, where Paul writes "what is sown in corruption is raised in incorruption" (1 Cor. 42–44). Corruption here does not mean moral turpitude. Rather it refers to the physical decomposition of the flesh. Irenaeus believed that God through Christ had healed our relationship with creation and reversed the process of decay. All of this would become manifest on the last day with the resurrection of the dead and the restoration of the entire creation.

Whereas for Origen Christ was seen as both a teacher and an ontological mediator, Christ for Irenaeus was the permanent expression of God's covenant with the whole creation. God became a human being not so much to teach us how to live and not so much (as in later Western theology) to pay a debt of guilt incurred by human sin. Instead, the Son of God became incarnate to divinize the creation and restore it to its incorruptible glory.[11] As Irenaeus writes in Book V of *Against the Heresies,* "Therefore [the Word of God] came in visible form into his own region (John 1:11) and was made flesh (1:14) and was hanged from the wood, in order to recapitulate everything in himself."[12] By "recapitulate" Irenaeus means that Christ undoes the sin of Adam and Eve and its subsequent disaster and re-founds the human race with Christ as the model of the new human. Christ is quite literally for Irenaeus the firstborn of a new humanity (see Col. 1:15–21). Irenaeus's anti-Gnosticism is extreme. Not only is the created world good; it is the intended dwelling of humans and the locus of a new and permanent covenant that God has made with the creation through the incarnation.

The full implications of Irenaeus's pro-material vision of salvation come toward the end of his treatise *Against the Heresies*. Here he paints a portrait of what the final restored creation will be like. His vision is a combination of images from the book of Isaiah and the book of Revelation. There will be, Irenaeus reminds his readers, "a new heaven and a new earth" and a new city Jerusalem "in which the just will experience imperishability and will prepare themselves for salvation."[13] This is not an allegory of spiritual things, on this Irenaeus is emphatic:

> none of this can be taken allegorically, but everything is solid and true and substantial, made by God for the enjoyment of just men. For as God is really the one who raises man, so man will really rise from the dead, and not allegorically.... And as he truly will rise, so also he will truly exercise imperishability and grow and be strong in the times of the kingdom.

Carrying this theme even further, Irenaeus reflects on the consequences of Christ's salvation: "Since men are real, their transformation must also be real, since they will not go into non-being but on the contrary will progress in being. For neither the substance nor the matter of the creation will be annihilated—true and solid is the one who established it."[14]

The anti-Gnostic physicality of Irenaeus's eschatological vision stands in sharp contrast with the anti-Gnostic spirituality of Origen's. Yet, although Irenaeus is a saint of the church and although his Pauline vision of redemption as freedom from corruption was a driving engine in the Trinitarian debates of the fourth century and the Christological debates of the fifth,[15] it was Origen's spirituality of ascent that dominated the subsequent tradition. Irenaeus's vision of the renewed material creation was a minority report in discourse dominated by champions of mystical ascent.[16]

The tale of the triumph of the Origenist style is aptly chronicled by Paul Santmire in his book *The Travail of Nature: The Ambiguous Ecological Promise of Christian Theology*.[17] According to Santmire, Christian thinking about nature has been dominated by two motifs. He calls these "the spiritual motif" and "the ecological motif." Origen is an example of the former, while Irenaeus is an example of the latter. When Christian theology, as with that of Origen, has been influenced by the spiritual motif, it tends to view the nonhuman creation as a means to an end, that is, as a temporary helper for humans en route to a spiritual destiny. When Christian theology has been influenced by the ecological motif, it tends to see the creation as the location for the entire project of salvation and, as such, as a necessary and indispensable part of that project.

Santmire locates the origin of the spiritual motif in what he calls the biblical experience of the overwhelming mountain. The classic example is Moses going up the mountain to converse with God and becoming lost in the mystery of divine power and otherness. The ecological motif, on the other hand, has root in the image of journey to the promised land, the land flowing with milk and honey, where God's covenant with Israel and with the land intertwine. Santmire argues that the image of the overwhelming mountain when detached from the image of the promising journey, creates a spirituality that images salvation as an ascent out of the world into the realm of the divine.[18] A full summary of Santmire's outstanding book is not necessary or possible here. What stands out, however, in his analysis is the extent to which the spiritual motif has been a dominant trope in the language of Western spirituality. Consider, for example some classic titles: John Climacus's *The Ladder of Divine Ascent,* St. John of the Cross's *Ascent of Mount Carmel,* or, more recently, Thomas Merton's *Seven Storey Mountain.* In all of these the image of ascent dominates.

In the classical spiritual tradition, the ascent of the spiritual mountain was also seen as a journey inward. The roots of this inward and upward journeying stem from the writings of the third-century Neo-Platonist Plotinus, but they find their way into Christian discourse through the writings of an anonymous author known as Pseudo-Dionysius. Dionysius's influence was vast: Bonaventure and Thomas Aquinas reflect strong threads of Dionysius's spirituality as do many other medieval authors. Even Gothic architecture, with its fascination with light, seems to have been impacted by the Dionysian idea of ascent to God through inward contemplation. Pseudo-Dionysius is one of the originators of the apophatic tradition, which states generally that we can know more about what God is not than we can know about what God is. *The Cloud of*

Unknowing, by an anonymous medieval author, reflects the spiritual judgments of Pseudo-Dionysius. Many modern Christians have been introduced to this spirituality through the popularization of *The Cloud of Unknowing* in and around the practice of centering prayer.

For Santmire, and for me, for all of its merits, this spiritual motif suffers from a number of limitations when applied to the task of constructing a theology of nature. In sum, it tends to present an overly spiritualized vision of human nature and human destiny. It is not my intention here to disparage the practice of centering prayer. In fact, it is a form or prayer that I personally enjoy very much and from which I have personally benefited a great deal; nevertheless, it is still possible to expose some of the limitations of its intellectual pedigree. Stated succinctly, the spiritual motif as expressed in many of the classical works of Christian spirituality runs the risk of encouraging a spirituality that is potentially world-denying.

This brings me full circle back to *Star Trek*. At the beginning of this essay I mentioned the Zalkonians who were, as a species, on the verge of evolving to a higher level of existence. One of the first to do so was the Zalkonian known as "John Doe" by the crew of the *Enterprise*. As the episode ends, John's material form dissolves: he mutates into pure energy and departs into space to embrace a future that is only implied. Now, in fairness, the transformed John is still a resident of this cosmos and presumably subject to the laws of physics. Still, the implication is clearly that the process of evolution leads from amino acids colliding in the primordial oceans of the earth, to the formation of simple organisms, to the rise of invertebrates, to vertebrates, to primates, to Lucy in the Rift valley of Kenya and Uganda, to early civilization, to modern civilization, to space-faring humanity, to humans who finally, in the words of World War II veteran and poet John Gillespie Maggee Jr., "slip the surly bonds of earth" and "touch the face of God."[19] *Star Trek* may have an overly optimistic view of humanity's teleology, but the idea that spirit is more desirable than matter has wide cultural support.

Yet most modern environmental theologians that I have read do not wish to slip the surly bonds of earth to touch the face of God. They would rather follow the pattern of Lyra Belacqua in Pullman's *His Dark Materials* and find themselves rooted to the earth in the centripetal pull of its material density. They would rather find God in and not apart from the material world. So great is the desire to identify with the divine energy at the center of all creation that they would rather lose their own particular identities to the ongoing project of life than ascend beyond the biosphere to contemplation of the divine being. They would rather have their atoms help construct the future generations of flowering plants and future coveys of creatures yet to evolve than to leave the rest of creation behind while they ascend beyond it in intellectual contemplation.[20]

There is in this worldview an emerging eco-spirituality, which rests upon a kind of ecological transcendentalism. This, I think, aptly describes the sentiment in Pullman's novels. Rather than transcending matter to spirit and achieving a fusion of identity with the being of God, as we find in much classical Christian mystical language, the religious imagery of this emerging spirituality suggests a transcendence back to matter. Our life dissolves back to the stardust from which we were formed. We are recycled into the project of life and by extension into the divine plan of the universe itself.

The resistance of many environmental theologians to the spiritual paradigm that has long dominated Christianity is difficult to overstate. On the one hand, this is understandable. There are indeed strong reasons to say that it lacks sufficient resources to respond to the actual environmental challenges that we face. If we see ourselves as spirits who are temporarily embodied and, as it were, "doing time" until we are liberated for a wholly spiritual destiny, it can be very difficult to view creation as anything other than a tool for our own spiritual progress. Rejecting this as an inadequate Christian view of nature makes great sense. I am surprised, however, by the number of Christian thinkers who have been willing to reject core Christian doctrines in the effort to embrace a less spiritualizing paradigm. For example many would argue that the omnipotence of God, the omniscience of God, the transcendence of God, the divinity of Jesus, the resurrection of the body, the resurrection of the person, the survival of individuality after death are all doctrines that are incompatible with an ecological paradigm. We see this most in a theological movement called process theology, but also to some extent in the writing of Passionist priest Thomas Berry (d. June 2009). Berry's essay *The Dream of the Earth* has influenced a whole generation of Christian eco-theologians. In the early '90s Berry teamed up with author Brian Swimme to publish a book called *The Universe Story: From the Primordial Flaring Forth to the Ecozoic Era — A Celebration of the Unfolding of the Cosmos*.[21] This book, and others, has spawned a popular movement called "the new cosmology," which, in my view, embraces a spirituality formally identical to that we encounter in Pullman's *His Dark Materials* series. It is in many ways lovely; it is romantic; it reflects a deep love of the earth and all creation. It seeks diligently to cultivate a new sense of reverence for all of creation and for the work of God in it. For these it is to be commended. In the process, however, this particular form of ecological spirituality sacrifices too much. In the end it lacks a coherent Christian core.

So then, what are we to do? If on the one hand we wish to avoid the world-denying tendency of the traditional paradigm of spirit ascending over matter but, on the other hand, not go down a path where we feel compelled to deny core Christian doctrines like the incarnation and the resurrection of the body, then we need to consider another model. In my view, that model exists within the resources of the tradition itself: we should work to recover and enhance the theological vision of Irenaeus.

The basic narrative of Irenaeus's theology is quite simple. God created a good world. Human beings were created to be a part of this world as their native environment. Human sin disrupted our relationships with each other, with God, and with the earth itself. Alienation and decay were the result of human rebellion. The incarnation of the Son of God delivers us from our alienation and restores us to a proper relationship with nature. The incarnation is God's permanent covenant with the whole creation. The prophetic expectation of the prophet Isaiah and the apocalyptic revelations of the book of Revelation point to a sure future where all of creation is renewed and endures in a kind of perpetual communion with God.

Now, Irenaeus's vision is, admittedly, mythic. Some object that it is wrong to suggest that we have a broken relationship with creation, or that there is something amiss with the trajectory of the natural world as we currently experience it. Far better, they suggest, to see nature — indeed the universe — as fundamentally fine and to define the spiritual task as accommodation to the limits of its reality. This, I think is the basic impulse of Thomas Berry, for example. Irenaeus, on the other hand, suggests that there is indeed something wrong, at least something wrong with our relationship with nature, and that we need to resist what is wrong by hoping for a different kind of future, a future where, to paraphrase Isaiah, the lion and the lamb will lie down and a little child will lead them.[22]

Irenaeus's intuition that something is wrong is profoundly Christian. This intuition reflects a deep and profound desire for justice. For Irenaeus, it is not that we need to adjust our attitudes to the givenness of reality; instead, God needs to fix what is broken in the reality that we encounter. In the latter years of his life, St. Augustine began to write in a very Irenaean way. Augustine scholar John Kenney describes this in his book *The Mysticism of St. Augustine.*[23] According to Kenney, Augustine was indeed heavily influenced by the same Neo-Platonism that produced what Santmire calls the spiritual motif, but, as he grew older, he began to return to the more physicalist paradigm of his youth, a paradigm that has roots in the earliest Christian movement and is expressed in the theology of Irenaeus. In *The City of God,* one of his most ambitious works, Augustine engages in a series of extended mediations on the afterlife. He wonders what will happen to our fingernails and hair clippings. He speculates about the endurance of gender: Will we be identifiably male and female in heaven? He asks if babies will rise as thirty-somethings and if old people will be young again.

All of these reflections strike modern readers as exceedingly odd. Indeed we could ask, where are they coming from? Why would he preach so literally about the characteristics of resurrected bodies? The answer can be found in one particular passage among these eschatological musings. In book 22 Augustine writes:

> Now we feel such extraordinary affection for the blessed martyrs that in the kingdom of God we want to see on their bodies the scars of the wounds which they suffered for Christ's name; and see them perhaps we shall. For in those wounds there will be no deformity, but only dignity, and the beauty of their valour will shine out, a beauty in the body and yet not of the body. And if the martyrs have had any limbs cut off, any parts removed, they will not lack those parts at the resurrection; for they have been told that "not a hair of your head will perish." But if it will be right that in that new age the marks of glorious wounds should remain in those immortal bodies, for all to see, then scars of the blows or the cuts will also be visible in

places where limbs were hacked off, although the parts have not been lost, but restored. And so the defects which have thus been caused in the body will no longer be there, in that new life; and yet, to be sure, those proofs of valour are not to be accounted defects, or to be called by that name.[24]

One could certainly interpret this passage as an overzealous probing into a future that cannot be known. Who, we might ask, cares that we can see the scars of the martyrs on their resurrected bodies? The answer, I think, is that we should all care because it is a matter of justice. Augustine's — and presumably his congregation's — desire to see scars on the bodies of people who inhabit the heavenly Jerusalem is, deep down, a desire that God give a final accounting for suffering. In Augustine's Irenaean heaven, the scars of the martyrs — the emblems of their suffering — have been transformed into glory. Their suffering has been redeemed.

If we consider Origen's paradigm in contrast, it is difficult to make sense of suffering. Origen understood our embodiment primarily as a means to facilitate a return to spiritual contemplation. In this model suffering is something of an annoyance that goads us to move beyond our materiality toward a deeper spiritual awareness. Suffering is like an itch that prompts us to scratch away the skin that distracts us from our true identity: it is pedagogical. Origen's view of suffering remains common. We often hear people say things like "suffering is a great teacher." This works for minor suffering, but is it an adequate way to deal with profound suffering such as we encounter all around the world. What possible lesson are people supposed to learn in, say, northern Uganda, Darfur, the Congo, or in any third world urban slum? Is the platitude "suffering is a great teacher" an adequate response to the parents who have lost a child in some random accident? Will it satisfy the victims of floods and violence and earthquakes and tsunamis? I think not.

In my view, the spiritual motif exemplified by Origen and the eco-mystical alternative fail to offer a coherent answer to suffering. In the latter model, suffering is explained as part of the growing pains of the emergent universe. Since God is seen to be intimately connected to this process, these growing pains are understood to be part of the suffering of God. Thus, all human suffering has meaning and purpose because it is a part of the drama of life and the infinite becoming of God. Yet, we could ask, is this really any different from explaining suffering as an itch to prompt spiritual awareness? Is it really enough to interpret the abysmal suffering of so many as part of the growing pains of the universe's becoming? In Dostoevsky's masterpiece *The Brothers Karamazov*, the suffering of a single child was enough to destroy the faith of brother Ivan, who rejected God for this reason alone. Is the universe's becoming a sufficient Christian response to the crushing realities that caused Ivan's rebellion, to Darfur, to Congo, to Haiti? Again, I think not.

If we seek an authentically Christian way to avoid the pitfalls associated with a spirituality of ascent, we can and should enhance our appreciation of the universe and work to recover a sense of awe in the face of its majesty. This is the real advantage of the eco-mysticism of people like Philip Pullman and Thomas Berry. On the other hand, if we want to ensure that we give an adequate account of suffering, we need something more. I suggest that the most promising dialogue partner for an emergent Irenaean eco-theology is liberation theology. Liberation theology orbits around a hunger and thirst for justice and the profound desire that God fix what has been broken. Liberation theologians and liberation practitioners labor for the realization of what Ignacio Ellacuría, S.J.— one of the Jesuits martyred in El Salvador in 1989—called the new society, a society marked by ubiquitous justice. Liberation theology is eschatologically ambiguous. On the one hand, it strives in the here and now for concrete instances of the promises of God. As the popular Catholic hymn intones, "Not in the dark of buildings confining, not in some heaven, light-years away, here in this place the new light is shining, now is the Kingdom, now is the day."[25] A theology of liberation demands liberation now and understands labor on behalf of this vision as a sacred duty of Christians. Yet, on the other hand, it recognizes that the full revelation of this vision will never be in the here and the now, but only in God's future, after the last day, in the heavenly Jerusalem. Our efforts here are an act of love and devotion to a vision of God's promise and our future. We see glimpses here, even at times solid concrete evidence, that the vision is real. There are real gains, there are also losses: the fullness of our hope eludes us and awaits its final revelation.

It seems to me that an expansion of the ambition of liberation theology to include the liberation of the whole creation has much potential. Just as we see our laboring on behalf of justice for the poor as sharing in God's building up of the kingdom of God, so also can we see our labors on behalf of the natural world caught up in this same purpose. If Irenaeus was correct to insist that the creation is the native place of humans, then it makes eminent sense to remind ourselves that the just society is not a place in the heavens, but a place on earth. Just as we must make an option for the poor in our daily discernments about a particular course of action, so also we should make a kind of option for the earth. The suffering of the earth caused by modern civilization is clearly not the same as the conscious suffering of human beings, but there is a way in which we can think of the two as connected. To the extent that we destroy the earth, we destroy the very conditions of our own existence and quite literally turn away (i.e., sin) from God's creative plan for life. The liberation of humanity from suffering and injustice and the liberation of the earth exist in parallel structures and point to a common hope. As Paul says, "We know that the whole creation has been groaning in labor pains until now; and not only the creation, but we ourselves, who have the first fruits of the Spirit, groan inwardly while we wait for the adoption, the redemption of our bodies" (Rom. 8:22–24). Perhaps in the heavenly Jerusalem we will see not just the glory of the scars of the martyrs, but also the glory of our wounded planet in its own redemption.

Notes

1. For a full discussion of this, see H. Paul Santmire, *The Travail of Nature: The Ambiguous Ecological Promise of Christian Theology* (Philadelphia: Fortress, 1985).

2. See John O'Keefe, "The Persistence of Grasmere: Contemporary Catholic Environmental Theology and the Romantic Impulse," *Journal of Religion and Society*, Supplement (2008).

3. John Milton, *Paradise Lost*, Book 2, lines 910–920.

4. Philip Pullman, *The Amber Spy Glass* (New York: Alfred A. Knopf, 2000), 319.

5. Information about the bishop's initiative on climate change and justice is available at *http://usccb.org/sdwp/ejp/climate/*.

6. See Arthur Lovejoy, *The Great Chain of Being: A Study of the History of an Idea* (Cambridge, Mass.: Harvard University Press, 1936).

7. See Robert Grant, *Irenaeus of Lyons* (London and New York: Routledge, 1997), 176–82.

8. Eusebius, *Ecclesiastical History* 6.8.

9. J. W. Trigg, *Origen: The Bible and Philosophy in the Third-Century Church* (Atlanta: John Knox, 1983) offers an excellent introduction to the life and contribution of Origen.

10. See David Dawson, *Christian Figural Reading and the Fashioning of Identity* (Berkeley: University of California Press, 2002).

11. The best discussion of this is Norman Russell, *The Doctrine of Deification in the Greek Patristic Tradition* (Oxford: Oxford University Press, 2004).

12. Grant, *Irenaeus of Lyons,* 170.

13. Ibid., 184.

14. Ibid.

15. I discuss this at some length in my article "The Persistence of Decay: Bodily Disintegration and Cyrillian Christology," in *In the Shadow of the Incarnation: Essays on Jesus Christ in the Early Church in Honor of Brian E. Daley, S.J.*, ed. Peter W. Martens (Notre Dame, Ind.: University of Notre Dame Press, 2008).

16. Although Caroline Walker Bynum argues persuasively that the doctrine of the resurrection of the body remained strong throughout the Middle Ages. See Caroline Walker Bynum, *The Resurrection of the Body in Western Christianity, 200–1336* (New York: Columbia University Press, 1995).

17. See note 1.

18. Santmire, *The Travail of Nature,* 1–29.

19. John Gillespie Maggee Jr., *High Flight, www.skygod.com/quotes/highflight.html* (accessed January 4, 2010).

20. See my discussion in "The Persistence of Grasmere," note 2 above.

21. Brian Swimme and Thomas Berry, *The Universe Story: From the Primordial Flaring Forth to the Ecozoic Era — A Celebration of the Unfolding of the Cosmos* (New York: HarperCollins, 1994).

22. This is more the approach recommended by John Haught in his book *Christianity and Science: Toward a Theology of Nature* (Maryknoll, N.Y.: Orbis Books, 2007).

23. John Peter Kenney, *The Mysticism of Saint Augustine* (New York: Routledge, 2005).

24. Augustine, *City of God,* trans. Henry Bettenson (New York: Penguin, 1884), book 22.19.

25. Marty Haugen, "Gather Us In" (Chicago: G.I.A. Publications, 1982).

FOUR

Environmental Degradation, Social Sin, and the Common Good

Jame Schaefer

WHILE REPORTS OF ENDANGERED SPECIES, pollutants and toxins in the environment, problematic nuclear and other hazardous wastes, and threats to the biosphere have been highlighted occasionally by the media for many years, recent attention has focused on changes that humans are forcing on the global climate. Indicators of these changes and dire predictions of adverse future effects have been identified periodically by the Intergovernmental Panel on Climate Change (IPCC), a collaborative effort of more than a thousand scholars amassed by the World Meteorological Organization and the United Nations Environment Programme to assess the latest scientific, technical, and socioeconomic studies so that well-informed decisions can be made to mitigate these effects.

Theologians also need to make some decisions, decisions that focus on ways in which we can contribute to the interdisciplinary dialogue that has emerged over the phenomenon of human-forced climate change. Since religions have the capacity to guide adherents in demonstrating the behavior needed to orient their lives toward the subjects of their worship, scholars of the world religions can identify teachings that might be helpful in addressing why some climate change-forcing behaviors should be avoided while others should be initiated.

Catholic theologians have much upon which to draw when addressing the damage that humans are causing one another, other species, and our planetary home. The data upon which we can rely span the Bible (the primary texts of our tradition), teachings over the centuries by eminent theologians who are revered in the Catholic tradition,[1] documents issued by the church magisterium, a growing array of theological reflections informed by scientific findings, and discussions of ethical imperatives pertaining to the natural environment. When read through an ecological lens, this rich combination of sources can be helpful and meaningful for addressing ecological degradation generally and human-forced climate change specifically.

Before discussing promising sources in the Catholic theological tradition, I summarize in the first section of this essay indications of change that humans are forcing on the global climate with emphasis on how the poor and vulnerable are affected. Two subsequent sections explore sequentially the sinfulness of individual and collective human actions that are thwarting the common good of God's Earth. These "social sins" demonstrate failure to love one's neighbor, violate Catholic social teaching's preferential option for the poor, and require our considering the "planetary common good." In the final section, I identify some basic commitments that must be made to reconcile with God for degrading Earth, point to some strategies aimed at mitigating the adverse effects on the climate that humans are forcing, and draw from Thomas Aquinas's understanding of cooperating grace that is available to embrace and implement these strategies. Implementing them will demonstrate our love for God by loving our neighbors in the most expansive sense, by showing our utmost concern for the poor and vulnerable humans and other constituents of Earth, and by striving to assure a sustainable and life-flourishing planet.

Environmental Degradation and Climate Change

Indicators of environmental degradation are abundant: the decline of biological diversity; the degradation and destruction of wetlands, coral reefs, forests, grasslands, and other ecological systems; pollutants and toxicants emitted into the air, flushed into waterways, and spread on the land; experimental and inadequately safeguarded technologies that decimate, injure, and genetically alter living entities and render areas uninhabitable for decades; highly radioactive and other hazardous wastes that accumulate without acceptable long-term solutions for disposal and isolation from the biosphere; relatively benign wastes that become problematic because of their sheer volume stemming from the prevailing throwaway mentality, especially in industrially developed countries; urban sprawl accompanied by increased automobile use that spews hydrocarbons into the air;[2] and "greenhouse" gases[3] produced by burning coal to generate electricity.

Adverse Effects of Human-forced Climate Change

Carbonic and nitrous compounds emitted into the air are highly problematic today because they are causing significant changes in the global climate.[4] While climatologists have found evidence to suggest that some extraterrestrial and terrestrial factors are primarily responsible for most of the past episodes of changes in Earth's climate,[5] these factors cannot account for the changes in the climate occurring today and predicted for the future.[6] A plethora of scientists have looked for other possible causes and have concluded that human input of carbonic and nitrous compounds into the atmosphere is responsible. The largest growth in greenhouse gas emissions between 1970 and 2004 came from energy production, other industries, and transportation, while residential and commercial buildings, forestry (including deforestation) and agriculture sectors grew at a lower rate.[7] Thus, we are "forcing" changes in our climate that exceed the effects caused by natural factors.[8]

Among these changes are increases in the average global air, land, and ocean temperatures in the Northern Hemisphere,[9] which are causing decreases in snow cover and thickness of sea ice, widespread melting of snow and ice,[10] rising sea level,[11] precipitation increases in eastern parts of North and South America, northern Europe, and northern and central Asia, precipitation declines in the Sahel (the narrow band of semi-arid land south of the Sahara Desert), the Mediterranean area, southern Africa, and parts of southern Asia,[12] changes in frequency and/or intensity of weather events over the last fifty years,[13] and increase in intense tropical cyclone activity in North America.[14]

These recent changes in the climate have adversely affected physical systems. For example, glacial lakes have enlarged and increased in numbers as glaciers and ice melts.[15] Ground instability has increased in permafrost regions while rock avalanches have increased in mountain regions.[16] Increased runoff is occurring in many glacier and snow-fed rivers. And lakes and rivers have warmed in many regions causing changes in the thermal structure of bodies of water and degraded water quality.[17]

Effects on biological systems are also significant. Within land systems, spring events (e.g., leaf unfolding and bird migration and egg laying) are occurring earlier, and ranges in plant and animal species are shifting upward.[18] Within marine and freshwater systems, rising water temperatures are causing higher levels of salinity, shifts in ranges of algal, plankton, and fish abundance, earlier fish migrations in rivers, and stresses on coral reefs.[19] The loss of coastal wetlands and mangroves is attributed to a combination of climate changes and human adaptations of these ecological systems.[20]

Adverse effects on human health from forced climate changes have also been detected. Among these are increased heat-related mortality in Europe, changes in infectious disease vectors in parts of Europe, and earlier onset of and increases in seasonal production of allergenic pollen in high and mid-latitudes of the Northern Hemisphere.[21]

Predictions of Future Effects

Scientists conclude that these and other effects will increase even if the emission of greenhouse gases is kept constant at levels that were recorded at the beginning of the twenty-first century. Continued greenhouse gas emissions at or above levels during the year 2000 would cause further warming and induce many changes in the global climate system during the twenty-first century that would "very likely" be larger than those observed during the twentieth century.[22] Among these changes are shrinking sea ice in the Arctic and Antarctic,[23] hot extremes in temperature, heat waves and heavy precipitation in high latitudes,[24] more intense tropical typhoons and hurricanes,[25] and increased flooding of coastal regions.

Predictions beyond the twenty-first century are more dire, even if greenhouse gas concentrations are constrained to current levels. Continuing to add current concentrations of greenhouse gases to the atmosphere would cause the sea level to rise for centuries due to the time scales associated with climate processes and feedbacks.[26] Prompted by the melting of glaciers and ice sheets on polar lands, the rising sea level would flood coastlines and inundate low-lying areas, the greatest effects of which will be in river deltas and low-lying islands.[27] Increasing atmospheric concentrations of greenhouse gases, especially carbon dioxide, will also further acidify the oceans.[28]

The survival of some species will also be threatened. According to the chairperson of the Intergovernmental Panel on Climate Change, approximately "20–30 percent of the species assessed in 2007 would be at increased risk of extinction if the global average temperature increase exceeds 1.5 to 2.5 degrees Centigrade," while an increase that exceeds about 3.5 degrees Centigrade suggests "significant extinctions" (40–70 percent of species assessed) around the planet.[29]

Also at risk are ecological systems whose ability to adapt to flooding, drought, wildfires, insect infestations, ocean acidification, and other disturbances caused by climate changes, particularly when these disturbances are combined with other drivers of ecological degradation, including land use changes, pollution, and overexploitation of natural sources. Major changes in the structure and function of ecological systems are anticipated with predominantly negative consequences for biological diversity and for water, food supply, clean air, and other goods.[30]

Adverse effects on ecological systems also put *Homo sapiens* at risk. According to the chairman of the Intergovernmental Panel on Climate Change, human-forced climate changes will have "serious effects on the sustainability of several ecosystems and the services they provide to human society."[31] A major anticipated effect on people is a decrease in the availability of water in the mid-latitudes and semi-arid areas of the planet. While an increase in water availability is anticipated in the moist tropics and at high latitudes, people in the Hindu-Kush, Himalaya, and Andes mountain ranges where more than one-sixth of the world's population currently lives will experience difficulty in obtaining the water they need, as will people in the Mediterranean Basin, western United States, southern Africa, northeastern Brazil, and other semi-arid areas. In already poverty-stricken Africa, between 75 million and 250 million people will be exposed to increased water stresses by the year 2020, including limited access to potable water.[32]

Food scarcity will also be exacerbated in many areas by the year 2020 due to a decline in crop productivity caused by changes in the global climate. Effects on crop productivity are particularly problematic in seasonally dry and tropical regions where it is projected to decrease with small local temperature increases of 1–2 degrees Centigrade. Yields from rain-fed agriculture in some African countries could be reduced by up to 50 percent.[33] While initial slight increases in crop productivity are projected at mid to high latitudes where the local average temperature rises from 1 to 3 degrees Centigrade, productivity is expected to decrease subsequently.[34] The same pattern of an initial increase in crop productivity followed by a decrease is anticipated globally.[35]

Millions more people are projected to experience yearly floods by the year 2080 due to sea level rise. Particularly vulnerable are mega-deltas of Asia whose major cities, including Shanghai, Dhaka, and Kolkata, cities on the coast, and cities in river flood plains where settlements, industries, and businesses are closely linked with climate-sensitive resources.[36] Small islands off Asia and Africa are especially vulnerable. Within these at-risk areas, poor communities will be most affected[37] because their sensitivity to the adverse effects of climate change is exacerbated by their poverty, food scarcity, malnutrition, and inaccessibility to other necessities of life. Adding to their impoverished circumstances, the poor are especially vulnerable to debilitating trends in economic globalization, regional conflicts, and diseases, including HIV/AIDS.[38]

The health of millions of people is also at risk as the global climate changes. Malnutrition, deaths, diarrheal and other diseases, injuries due to extreme weather events, and increased frequency of cardio-respiratory diseases caused by higher concentrations of ground-level ozone in urban areas are included in these projections.[39] While residents in temperate areas may benefit initially by fewer deaths from cold exposure and combinations of other factors,[40] any benefits will be outweighed by the negative health effects of rising temperatures, especially in developing countries.[41] Poor people are most vulnerable to adverse health effects caused by forced climate change. Education, health care programs, and public health initiatives are crucial for shaping healthy populations to prevent more adverse effects.[42]

When accepting the 2007 Nobel Peace Prize on behalf of the Intergovernmental Panel on Climate Change, Chairman Rajendra Pachauri underscored the equity implications of climate change and how they will affect some of the poorest and most vulnerable communities of the world:

> One of the most significant aspects of the impacts of climate change, which has unfortunately not received adequate attention from scholars in the social sciences, relates to the equity implications of changes that are occurring and are likely to occur in the future. In general, the impacts of climate change on some of the poorest and the most vulnerable communities in the world could prove extremely unsettling. And, given the inadequacy of capacity, economic strength, and institutional capabilities characterizing some of these communities, they would remain extremely vulnerable to the impacts of climate change and may, therefore, actually see a decline in their economic condition, with a loss of livelihoods and opportunities to maintain even subsistence levels of existence.[43]

Pachauri also called attention to the potential conflicts resulting from human-forced climate change and lamented the IPCC's failure to provide directions for mitigating them. He expressed concern about conflicts that may arise when access to clean water, food availability, stable health conditions, ecosystem resources, and secure settlements are disrupted by changes in the climate.[44] A major potential source of conflict that the IPCC chairman identified is the migration and movement of people from one area to another.[45] Though usually temporary and often from rural to urban areas in response to floods, famine, and warfare, the migration and movement of people from adverse impacts of climate change may become highly problematic for them, for the people of the regions to which they are relocating, and for efforts to establish a peaceful global society. To address these potential threats, Pachauri urged conducting an "in-depth analysis of risks to security among the most vulnerable sectors and communities impacted by climate change across the globe."[46]

From Social Sin to Planetary Sin

These indicators of environmental problems generally and human-forced climate change particularly have significance for how we think about ourselves as God's faithful people and how we demonstrate our faith. Much has been written about "sin" by leaders and scholars of Catholic and other Abrahamic traditions who generally consider sin a personal offense against God in which we abuse the freedom given to us by failing to love God and others.[47] Much more has been written about different kinds of sin, all of which point to the personal culpability of the individual.

In recent decades, some moral theologians have turned their attention to the social dimensions of sin. Latin American bishops and liberation theologians prompted much of this focus when responding to people in their midst who were struggling to survive under oppressive regimes and repressive socioeconomic structures.[48] Bishops and theologians continue to strive for a more comprehensive understanding of human sinfulness and to identify wrongly ordered patterns of human behavior that have become institutionalized. When these patterns of behavior become institutionalized, moral theologian Margaret Pfeil contends rightly, people tend to "succumb to a kind of moral blindness whereby they participate in their societal institution or system without realizing that their actions, both of commission and omission, contribute to structures of sin."[49] Eventually, the phrase "social sin" emerged in magisterial teachings of the church and in the works of moral theologians, though bishops and popes have underscored personal sin as the root of social sin.

In the *Catechism of the Catholic Church*, the bishops of the United States describe "sin" as "a personal act" for which the individual is responsible. However, they continue,

> [W]e have a responsibility for the sins committed by others when *we cooperate in them*:
>
> — by participating directly and voluntarily in them;
>
> — by ordering, advising, praising, or approving them;
>
> — by not disclosing or not hindering them when we have an obligation to do so; [and]
>
> — by protecting evil-doers.[50]

Thus, the bishops teach, "sin makes men accomplices of one another and causes concupiscence, violence, and injustice to reign among them."[51] From the bishops' perspective, at least implicitly, sin becomes a cooperative endeavor that can involve many.

Sin also gives "rise to social situations and institutions that are contrary to the divine goodness," the bishops contend. "These 'structures of sin' are expressions and effects of personal sins that lead their victims to do evil in their turn. Thus, in an analogous sense, structures of sin constitute a sin of society, a 'social sin.'"[52]

When judging structures of sin in society as socially sinful, United States Catholic bishops were following the teachings of the late Pope John Paul II, who named and explained "social sin" in *Reconciliatio et paenitentia* (On Reconciliation and Penance), an apostolic exhortation issued in 1984.[53] According to the pope, a social sin has three dimensions:

1. an individual's personal sin that affects others;

2. an offense against God because the individual offends his or her neighbor — an offense that applies to every sin against justice in interpersonal relationships that is *committed* or *omitted* either by the individual against the community or by the community against the individual, against the rights of the human person, against the freedom of others, against the dignity and honor of one's neighbor, and against the common good, which includes "the whole broad spectrum of the rights and duties of citizens";

3. a relationship among various human communities that do not accord with God's plan for justice in the world and freedom and peace between individuals, groups, and peoples.[54]

While these social sins may appear anonymous, the pope continued, they are rooted, nevertheless, in personal sin:

> Whenever the church speaks of situations of sin or when [she] condemns as social sins certain situations or the collective behavior of certain social groups, big or small, or even of whole nations and blocs of nations, she knows and she proclaims that such cases of social sin are the result of the accumulation and concentration of many personal sins... of

those who cause or support evil or who exploit it; of those who are in a position to avoid, eliminate, or at least limit certain social evils but who fail to do so out of laziness, fear, or the conspiracy of silence, through secret complicity or indifference; of those who take refuge in the supposed impossibility of changing the world and also of those who sidestep the effort and sacrifice required, producing specious reasons of higher order. The real responsibility, then, lies with individuals.[55]

Interestingly, John Paul II prefaced his description of social sin with an explanation that human sin constitutes a refusal "to submit to God," resulting in the destruction of the person's "internal balance" and causing "contradictions and conflicts" to arise. He underscored his thinking that the individual who commits a social sin damages his or her relationship with others *and with the created world:*

Wounded in this way, man almost inevitably causes damage to the fabric of his relationship with others and with the created world. This is an objective law and an objective reality, verified in so many ways in the human psyche and in the spiritual life as well as in society, where it is easy to see the signs and effects of internal disorder.[56]

From a Catholic, Christian perspective, should acts that accelerate the extinction of species, degrade the air regimes, landmasses, and waterways, and threaten a life-sustaining climate be categorized as "social sins"? Are they social sins because so many of the problems we are causing are adversely affecting our neighbors near and far in the present? Are they social sins because our actions will inevitably affect our neighbors in the future who have not caused these adversities either directly or indirectly? Are they social sins because the poorest and most vulnerable people are most susceptible to being adversely affected by environmental degradation generally and by human-forced climate change particularly? Are they social sins because degrading the natural environment violates the common good of humanity by threatening the internal integrity of God's Earth?

While we can respond positively to each of these questions, we can ponder whether or not "social sin" is the best category for acts that threaten other species, destroy their habitats, disrupt the functioning of ecological systems, and force changes to the biosphere's climate. Pope John Paul II's recognition that social sin "almost inevitably causes damage to the fabric of [our] relationship with others and with the created world"[57] opens to another category for thinking about the sinfulness of ecological degradation as damaging our relationship with Earth, its ecological systems, and other species. That we are damaging Earth by forcing changes in the global climate cannot be ignored. By damaging it, we are thwarting the life-sustaining capability of our planet, our temporal home that we share with other species, their habitats, and ecological systems.

Thus, a more inclusive category is needed. "Planetary sin" seems more appropriate. Whereas the category of *social sin* tends to limit the effects of sin to humans and our interrelationships, the category of planetary sin encompasses all types of sins that injure others, our relationships with them, and, ultimately, our relationship with God. Of course, the adverse effects of human-forced climate change on other species and biological systems also affect our species in one way or another, now and in the future. Nevertheless, referring to actions that cause such pervasive havoc in Earth's functioning as sins of a planetary magnitude is more cogent, and the category of planetary sin can be understood as incorporating social sins that affect other humans in their societal relationships. When viewed from this perspective, planetary sin becomes an all-encompassing category of human sinfulness and underscores our culpability for actions or inactions — commission and omission — that adversely affect more than human constituents of Earth.

A sticky question arises, nevertheless, when attempting to frame the culpability of humans who are enmeshed in the structures of planetary sin. While we must acknowledge our culpability for *planetary sins of omission* when failing to take action in our daily lives that would help mitigate climate change, and we must also acknowledge our culpability for *planetary sins of commission,* whereby we directly and/or indirectly engage in activities that force climate change, to what extent are we culpable for actions that are embedded in the socioeconomic structures of planetary sin (e.g., purchasing packaged foods produced and transported over long distances to their markets and using electricity produced from burning dirty coal)? At the very least, culpability can be lessened by remaining open to information about the adverse effects of actions we are contemplating, choosing alternatives that are available at all socioeconomic levels in which we are engaged, and urging the increased availability of alternatives that do not cause adversities. Culpability can also be lessened by promoting legislation at appropriate local to international levels that will mitigate the effects of social, economic, and political structures of sin.

Failing to take action, individually and, where warranted, collectively to mitigate harm to humans, other species, and to the air, land, and waters constitutes planetary sins of omission that offend God. These sins offend God because they constitute failures to love our human neighbors — the social aspect of planetary sins. When we fail to love our neighbors, theologian Karl Rahner taught, we are failing to love God.[58] Our failure to love the poor and vulnerable and to have preference for them in our individual and collective decision making and actions is particularly offensive.

These planetary sins also offend God because they adversely affect God's ongoing creation. Planetary sins offend God, the creator and sustainer of the world, who values the world (as the inspired Priestly writer proclaimed in Genesis 1), who loves the world (as John the Evangelist proclaimed), and who has a purpose for the world that we would be much too presumptuous to identify (as theologian John Haught cautions).[59]

Since humans are so interconnected with other species and abiota in the dynamic web of life, so related to them through the evolutionary process out of which our species emerged from and with them, and so radically dependent upon them for our temporal needs and well-being, we cannot think about the fate of humans apart from the fate of other species, ecological systems, and the biosphere. What affects them, affects us. We are all affected because together we constitute a mutual community that is Earth. We are Earth constituents, and we have a common temporal good — a life-sustaining planet. That our planet retains the capacity of internally sustaining itself as a unity of diverse constituents is our shared common good.

How solid is this notion of the "common good" from an ecological perspective as a mutual good shared by all constituents of Earth? We turn to St. Thomas Aquinas, the great thirteenth century systematic theologian, for his insight while informing his teachings with current scientific findings.

The Planetary Common Good

While the phrase "the common good" has been used primarily by the teaching authority of the church and by theologians to refer to the common good of people,[60] Aquinas established an understanding of the common good that was cosmic in scope. We may have lost that sense of the cosmic common good for several centuries, but ecological problems and particularly climate changes we are forcing require its retrieval and consideration today when faced with threats to our planetary common good.

What is the cosmic common good? Aquinas expounded systematically on the goodness of the universe that is demonstrated by the orderly functioning of its constituents in relation to one another. From his understanding of the value that each type of creature brings to this functioning, he glowingly described the unity brought about by their orderly interactivity as the greatest created good,[61] the highest perfection of the created world,[62] and its most beautiful attribute.[63] The order of things to one another is the nearest thing to God's goodness because every particular good is ordered to the good of the whole.[64] That some things exist for the sake of others and also for the sake of the perfection of the universe is not contradictory since some are needed by others to maintain the internal integrity of the universe and all things are needed to contribute to its perfection.[65] When all parts function in relation to one another in innately appropriate ways as intended by God, the universe is indeed perfect, reflects God's goodness, and manifests God's glory.[66]

Thus, the good of the whole — the common good — is the internal sustainability and integrity of the universe. From Aquinas's perspective, God instilled in each creature a natural inclination toward the common good.[67] Each creature is more strongly inclined to the common good than to itself and that inclination is demonstrated by its operation.[68] For example, sometimes a creature suffers damage to itself for the sake of the common good.[69] At the root of this appetite for the common good is the natural inclination each creature has for God, who is the absolute common good of all creatures.[70]

God is the uncreated common good whereas the internal integrity of the universe is its created common good to which all parts, including human creatures, are oriented in their temporal lives. While all parts are inclined toward the common good of the whole, creatures that have a greater capacity to act have a greater appetite for the common good and are inclined to seek to do good for others far removed from them.[71] Human creatures have the capacity to make and execute informed decisions. If the person does not will a particular good for the common good, that willful act is not right.[72]

Because humans often act incorrectly by not directing their wills toward the common created good and ultimately toward the common uncreated Good, who is God, God cares providentially for humans by offering them grace to help them exercise their wills appropriately in temporal life with a view toward their ultimate goal of eternal life with God.[73] God's grace both operates on and cooperates with humans toward their ultimate goal[74] without interfering in the human exercise of freely making and carrying out decisions.[75] God's grace operates lovingly on the human spirit so the individual thinks and acts in ways that are conducive to achieving eternal life.[76] God's grace cooperates with the individual by actively sustaining the innate human capacity to make informed decisions and to choose to act accordingly. God's grace also operates on and cooperates with humans to develop moral virtues that will aid them in exercising their wills appropriately to achieve the common good in this life because they are motivated to achieve eternal life with God.[77]

Nevertheless, all entities that constitute the universe benefit from being moved toward the common good of the whole, Aquinas reasoned.[78] Using a parallel example of the leader of an army, he maintained that the ordering of all parts to the good of the whole is what a leader of an army does when intending their mutual good.[79] They all benefit from the ordering of parts to one another, which enables them to function appropriately to bring about the good of the whole.[80]

Aquinas insisted that God intends all creatures to cooperate for the good of the whole. In the operations of nonintellectual creatures, harmony and actions that are conducive to the realization of the common good almost always prevail because they are directed by God to achieve their purposes according to their natures.[81] Creatures who are gifted with the ability to think and to exercise their wills freely are also intended to will the common good.[82] As Legrand observed from Aquinas's teachings, no part of creation or type of creature is excluded from God's intention that all cooperate, combine, or harmonize within the order of the universe, an order established by God to maintain its internal functioning through which it achieves the good that is common to all.[83]

When Aquinas contended that creatures cooperate in securing the common good, he was not only thinking about creatures cooperating among themselves within the hierarchy of creatures to assure their mutual sustainability in this life as God intends. He also considered the inter-cooperation of creatures as cooperating with God. He insisted that creatures who are endowed with greater capacities to act (e.g., to reason and make informed decisions) are intended to cooperate with God in acquiring the good of the whole universe. Unless more endowed creatures cooperate in procuring the good of less capable creatures, the abundance of goodness would be confined to an individual or only a few.[84] The good of many is better than the good of an individual, he continued, and the good of the universe as a whole is best because it is more representative of God's goodness.

Furthermore, according to Aquinas, goodness becomes common to many through the cooperation of more capable creatures.[85] More capable creatures are expected to cooperate in seeking the good of others. Creatures cooperate with one another for the good of the whole, Aquinas maintained, because they are related to God as their creator. God ordered creatures to one another to achieve their internal common good of sustaining themselves as an integral whole. In one of his most succinct treatments of this subject, he explained that the entire universe of interconnected parts achieves its purpose when all parts function in relation to one another in ways that are appropriate to the innate characteristics of each part.[86] Their *created* common good is the good of the whole order of creatures functioning in appropriate, relational ways to sustain themselves as intended by God while aiming toward eternity with God, who is the *uncreated* common good of the entire universe. Furthermore, functioning in these relational ways best manifests God's goodness and gives glory to God.[87]

As French contends astutely, Aquinas's concept of the common good provides a "cosmological-ecological principle" for his ethical system,[88] which is helpful today when viewed from the perspective of environmental degradation in general and human-forced climate change in particular. The good sought in common would be the good of ecological systems of which humans are integral actors who rely on other interacting biota and abiota for their health and well being. This ethical framework of the common good for addressing environmental issues also appeals to Longwood, who recognizes the need to remain cognizant of human existence in the "complex and subtly balanced system of the web of life" in which all parts function to maintain the quality of the integrated whole.[89]

How can the planetary common good be sought? Basically, the internal flourishing of Earth can be sought by humans making a commitment in solidarity with one another to function in solidarity with all constituents of Earth. That our species is interconnected materially with other species cannot be denied in light of evolutionary and molecular biological findings. That our species is interconnected with other species, the land, air, and water in ecosystems is well documented by ecosystem science. Yet a commitment to solidarity with them and the systems within which humans are integral actors requires more. A commitment to solidarity with other species, abiota, and systems also requires our valuing them intrinsically for themselves outside of their usefulness to us, striving to understand how species and abiota relate to one another, and valuing their interrelationships. Furthermore, a commitment to solidarity assumes a foremost concern for the poor, who are most vulnerable to environmental degradation in general and the adverse effects of human-forced climate change in particular.

Reconciliation to Achieve the Planetary Common Good

How should we commit ourselves to the planetary common good? As Pope John Paul II urged, we should commit ourselves with "a firm and persevering determination." Three related commitments are needed.

1. *A commitment to examine our personal attitudes and actions in relation to others — other humans now and into the future, other species, ecological systems, and the biosphere — with the aim of*

discerning how we are contributing to the degradation of Earth generally and to climate change specifically in our social, economic, and political activities. We need to view ourselves realistically, as constituents among other diverse constituents in the dynamic web of existence who eschew any sense of sovereignty over others, who recognize their distinctiveness, who are open to opportunities for making informed decisions about how to function in ways that achieve the planetary common good, and who execute these decisions firmly.

2. *A commitment to draw upon our individual spiritual and moral capacities to bring about our conversion to the planetary common good out of love for God and love for our neighbors when "neighbor" is understood in the most expansive and altruistic sense to include other species and biological systems.* We need to develop in ourselves individually and collaboratively the moral virtues of prudence, justice, moderation, fortitude, and solidarity motivated by love for God and love for our neighbors. We need to discern practices and policies that are conducive to the planetary common good. We need to implement these policies and practices with a firm sense of justice for all to obtain what they need to sustain their lives. We need to be particularly concerned about the poor and vulnerable humans who are most affected by environmental degradation generally and human-forced climate change particularly, and we must show preference to their well-being so they are able to cope with changes that are affecting them. We also need to be concerned about and give preference for other species whose existence is threatened since they are, as theologian Sallie McFague characterizes them, the "new poor" of our planet.[90]

3. *A commitment to act individually and collaboratively for the planetary common good to remedy the structures of planetary sin that thwart the internal sustainability of Earth.* Following the principle of subsidiarity, we need to work concurrently at all levels of decision making to minimize the adverse effects that our actions are causing. Mitigating strategies are needed in our homes, in our places of employment, in our schools, in our industries, in our recreational activities, and in our governments. We need to implement strategies that we can control directly while advocating strategies that need to be implemented by employers and policy-makers at various levels of governance. We need to think and act both locally and globally in

light of the dire predictions through promising means of thwarting these predictions. While local and national decisions on strategies aimed at mitigating climate changes may be difficult and advocates favoring these strategies must be well-informed and persistent, decisions made at the international level may be even more difficult as nations protect their self-interests amid complicating contexts of economic instability and terrorist activities. Their cooperation to seek the planetary common good is absolutely vital,[91] especially in light of the high degree of confidence that IPCC specialists have in environmentally effective, cost-effective, equitably distributable, technologically diffuse, and institutionally feasible strategies that may reduce global greenhouse gases.[92] And, we need to persist in urging nations to focus on promising strategies that aim to achieve the mutual good of all people.

Conclusion

As people of faith in God, who continually self-communicates to us, we can be confident that God's grace is available to us to keep these commitments. We need to remain open to receiving God's grace and to cooperating with God by working to overcome planetary sins and by seeking the common good of all Earth's constituents. By opening to, receiving, and cooperating with God's grace,[93] we will be fortified to support and act on adaptation and mitigation strategies that are aimed at minimizing the adverse effects of human-forced climate change.

Some adaptation strategies may be effective (e.g., moving away from coasts and flood plains, retrofitting and building dwellings that can withstand extremes in temperatures and weather phenomena), though these strategies must be carefully planned and executed to avoid catastrophic events (e.g., mass migrations) and to help people for whom these strategies are problematic (e.g., the elderly, the infirm, and the poor, for whom we must show preference). While little information is available about the costs and effectiveness of adaptation measures, many studies have focused on mitigation strategies[94] that are aimed at reducing greenhouse gas emissions in all sectors of the economy and society. The IPCC's Working Group III enumerates benefits that can result from greenhouse gas reduction strategies, including health co-benefits, local economic benefits in the form of development, poverty alleviation, employment, energy security, and local environmental protection.[95]

The possibility that changes in behavior patterns can contribute to mitigating human-forced climate change should encourage us to initiate actions in our own homes, places of employment, and local communities. Changes in consumption patterns, changes in occupying buildings, changes in our modes of transportation, and changes in business practices are changes that each of us can make individually and in collaboration with others. Thus, we need not feel helpless in practice. Nor should we feel helpless as we contend with our present and face our future, bolstered by our confidence in God to grace our commitments to mitigate the adverse effects of human-forced climate change and move cooperatively toward the planetary common good — a life-sustaining and flourishing planet.

Notes

1. For promising patristic and medieval concepts that are ripe for retrieval, reconstruction, and application to ecological problems, see Jame Schaefer, *Theological Foundations for Environmental Ethics: Reconstructing Patristic and Medieval Concepts* (Washington D.C.: Georgetown University Press, 2009).

2. Summarized from scientific reports in ibid., 203–11.

3. The primary "greenhouse" gases include carbon dioxide, methane, nitrous oxide, and ozone, which trap heat within the lower atmosphere (troposphere) of our planet.

4. Intergovernmental Panel on Climate Change, *Climate Change 2007: Synthesis Report, Contribution of Working Groups I, II, and III to the Fourth Assessment Report,* ed. Rajendra K. Pachauri and Andy Reisinger (Geneva: Intergovernmental Panel on Climate Change, 2008); hereafter IPCC, *Climate Change 2007: Synthesis Report.* This report is also accessible from *www.ipcc.ch/publications_and_data/ publications_ipcc_fourth _assessment_report_synthesis_report.htm.*

5. Extraterrestrial factors include solar output, Earth-Sun geometry, and interstellar dust, while terrestrial factors from oceans, the atmosphere, and land include volcanic emissions, mountain-building, continental drift, atmospheric chemistry, atmospheric reflectivity, land reflectivity, and atmosphere/ocean heat exchange. See discussion at "Factors that influence the Earth's climate," PhysicalGeography.net, *www.physicalgeography.net/fundamentals/7y.html* (accessed September 9, 2009).

6. IPCC, *Climate Change 2007: Synthesis Report.*

7. Ibid., 36.

8. A succinct overview of conclusive evidence pointing to anthropogenic causes of climate change is provided in the IPCC's *Climate Change 2007: Synthesis Report.*

9. IPCC, *Climate Change 2007: Synthesis Report, Summary for Policy Makers,* Working Group I, 3.2, 3.4, 5.2 Average Arctic temperatures have increased at almost twice the global average rate in the past hundred years. Land regions have warmed faster than the oceans. Observations since 1961 show that the average temperature of the global ocean has increased to depths of at least three thousand meters and that the ocean has been taking up over 80 percent of the heat being added to the climate system. New analyses of balloon-borne and satellite measurements of lower- and mid-tropospheric temperature show warming rates similar to those observed in surface temperature. Working Group II concluded from more than 29,000 observational data series collected in 75 studies showing significant changes in many physical and biological systems that more than 89 percent are consistent with the direction of change expected as a response to warming. This report is also accessible from *www.ipcc.ch/pdf/assessment-report/ar4/syr/ar4_syr_spm.pdf.*

10. According to Working Group I, at 3.2, 4.5, 4.6, 4.7, 4.8, 5.5 in IPCC, *Climate Change 2007: Synthesis Report, Summary for Policy Makers,* decreases in snow and ice extent are also consistent with warming (Figure 1.1). Satellite data since 1978 show that annual average Arctic sea ice extent has shrunk by 2.7 [2.1 to 3.3] percent per decade, with larger decreases in summer of 7.4 [5.0 to 9.8] percent per decade. Mountain glaciers and snow cover on average have declined in both hemispheres. The maximum areal extent of seasonally frozen ground has decreased by about 7 percent in the Northern Hemisphere since 1900, with decreases in spring of up to 15 percent. Temperatures at the top of the permafrost layer have generally increased since the 1980s in the Arctic by up to 3 degrees Celsius.

11. IPCC, *Climate Change 2007: Synthesis Report,* 30. See also Working Group I, 4.6, 4.8, and 5.5 in *Summary for Policy Makers* on the consistency of increases in sea level with global warming (Figure 1.1). Global average sea level rose at an average rate of 1.8 [1.3 to 2.3] millimeters per year over 1961 to 2003 and at an average rate of about 3.1 [2.4 to 3.8] millimeters per year from 1993 to 2003. Whether this faster rate for 1993 to 2003 reflects decadal variation or an increase in the longer term trend is unclear. Since 1993 thermal expansion of the oceans has contributed about 57 percent of the sum of the estimated individual contributions to the sea level rise, with decreases in glaciers and

ice caps contributing about 28 percent and losses from the polar ice sheets contributing the remainder. From 1993 to 2003 the sum of these climate contributions is consistent within uncertainties with the total sea level rise that is directly observed.

12. IPCC, *Climate Change 2007: Synthesis Report, Summary for Policy Makers,* Working Group I, 3.3 and 3.9.

13. For example, cold days, cold nights, and frosts have become less frequent and/or have changed in intensity over most land areas while hot days, hot nights, and heat waves have become more frequent. See IPCC, *Climate Change 2007: Synthesis Report, Summary for Policy Makers,* Working Group I, 3.8 and 3.9.

14. IPCC, *Climate Change 2007: Synthesis Report, Summary for Policy Makers,* Working Group I, 3.8, from observations since 1970.

15. IPCC, *Climate Change 2007: Synthesis Report, Summary for Policy Makers,* Working Group II, 1.3.

16. Ibid.

17. Ibid., 15.2.

18. IPCC, *Climate Change 2007: Synthesis Report, Summary for Policy Makers,* Working Group II, 1.3, 8.2, and 14.2.

19. IPCC, *Climate Change 2007: Synthesis Report, Summary for Policy Makers,* Working Group II, 1.3. However, separating climate change stresses on coral reefs from other stresses (e.g., overfishing and pollution) is difficult.

20. IPCC, *Climate Change 2007: Synthesis Report,* 33. See also *Summary for Policy Makers,* Working Group II, 1.3, 1.

21. IPCC, *Climate Change 2007: Synthesis Report,* 33. See also *Summary for Policy Makers,* Working Group II, 1.3, 8.2, and 8.ES.

22. IPCC, *Climate Change 2007: Synthesis Report,* 45.

23. IPCC, *Climate Change 2007: Synthesis Report, Summary for Policy Makers,* Working Group I, 10.3, Figure 3.2.

24. IPCC, *Climate Change 2007: Synthesis Report, Summary for Policy Makers,* Table 3.2. In most subtropical land regions, decreases are likely, thus continuing current trends, as reported by Working Group I, 3.3, 8.3, 9.5, 10.3 and 11.2–11.9.

25. IPCC, *Climate Change 2007: Synthesis Report, Summary for Policy Makers,* Working Group I, 3.8, 9.5 and 10.3. Continuing the broad pattern over the last fifty years, extra-tropical storm tracks are projected to move poleward, with consequent changes in wind, precipitation, and temperature patterns. WGI 3.6, 10.3, SPM.

26. IPCC, *Climate Change 2007: Synthesis Report,* 46. See also *Summary for Policy Makers,* Working Group I, 10.4, 10.5 and 10.7.

27. R. K. Pachauri, Chairman, IPCC, "Acceptance Speech for the Nobel Peace Prize Awarded to the Intergovernmental Panel on Climate Change (IPCC)," Oslo, Norway, December 10, 2007. Accessible from *www.ipcc.ch/graphics/speeches/nobel-peace-prize-oslo-10-december-2007 .pdf*. Hereafter, Pachauri, "Acceptance Speech."

28. IPCC, *Climate Change 2007: Synthesis Report,* 52.

29. IPCC Chairman, Rajendra Pachauri, Opening Session of the World Economic Forum, Davos, Switzerland, January 23, 2008, *www.ipcc.ch/graphics/speeches/pachauri-davos-january-2008.pdf*. Hereafter, Pachauri, World Economic Forum.

30. IPCC, *Climate Change 2007: Synthesis Report, Summary for Policy Makers,* Working Group II, 4.4, Box TS.6.

31. Pachauri, "Acceptance Speech."

32. Ibid.

33. Ibid.

34. IPCC, *Climate Change 2007: Synthesis Report, Summary for Policy Makers,* Working Group II, 5.4.

35. Ibid., and 5.5.

36. Pachauri, World Economic Forum. See also IPCC, *Climate Change 2007: Synthesis Report, Summary for Policy Makers,* Working Group II, 6.3, 6.4, 7.1, 7.3, 7.4 and 7.5.

37. IPCC, *Climate Change 2007: Synthesis Report, Summary for Policy Makers,* Working Group II, 7.2, 7.4 and 5.4.

38. Pachauri, "Acceptance Speech."

39. IPCC, *Climate Change 2007: Synthesis Report, Summary for Policy Makers,* Working Group I, 7.4, Box 7.4, and Working Group II, 8.2 and 8.4.

40. Ibid.

41. IPCC, *Climate Change 2007: Synthesis Report, Summary for Policy Makers,* Working Group II, 8.4, 8.7, and 8ES.

42. Ibid., 8.3.

43. Pachauri, "Acceptance Speech."

44. Ibid.

45. Ibid.

46. Ibid.

47. United States Catholic Conference, *Catechism of the Catholic Church* (Washington D.C.: United States Catholic Conference, 1994) #387, 97. Other nuances of this definition of "sin" included in the *Catechism* are sin as an offense against reason, truth, and right conscience, sin as a failure in genuine love for God and neighbor caused by a perverse attachment to certain goods (#1849), and sin as an offense against God

that sets oneself against God's love and turns one's heart away from God's love (#1850).

48. Margaret R. Pfeil, "Social Sin: Social Reconciliation?" in *Reconciliation, Nations and Churches in Latin America*, ed. Iain Maclean (Burlington, Vt.: Ashgate, 2006), 171–89 at 172.

49. Ibid.

50. United States Catholic Conference, *Catechism of the Catholic Church* (Washington, D.C.: United States Catholic Conference, 1994), #1868–69, 457.

51. Ibid.

52. Ibid.

53. John Paul II, *Reconciliatio et paenitentia*, Apostolic Exhortation, December 2, 1984, *www.vatican.va*.

54. Ibid.

55. Ibid.

56. Ibid.

57. John Paul II, *Reconciliatio et paenitentia*.

58. Karl Rahner, "Reflections on the Unity of Love of Neighbour and the Love of God," in *Theological Studies* 6, trans Karl-H. and Boniface Kruger, 231–49 (New York: Crossroad, 1982).

59. John 1:3; John F. Haught, *Science and Religion: From Conflict to Conversation* (New York: Paulist,1995), 180–82.

60. David Hollenbach, S.J., *The Common Good and Christian Ethics* (Cambridge UK: Cambridge University Press, 2002).

61. Aquinas, *Summa contra Gentiles* 2.39; see further 2.44, 2.45, 3.69, and 3.144. Also see *Summa theologiae* 1.15.2 and 1.22.1–2.

62. Aquinas, *Summa contra Gentiles* 2.45; see further 2.44.

63. Aquinas, *Summa contra Gentiles* 3.71. The universe cannot be any better than it is, he wrote in *Summa theologiae* 1.25.6 ad 3, because of the most beautiful order given to things by God. As John H. Wright concludes in *The Order of the Universe in the Theology of St. Thomas Aquinas* (Rome: Apud Aedes Universitatis Gregorianae, 1957), 87, the universe is "God's masterpiece" with its excellence found in the ordered harmony of its parts.

64. Aquinas, *Summa contra Gentiles* 3.64 and 112. See also *Summa theologiae* 1.47.2. The integrity of all created beings is described in *Summa contra Gentiles* 2.45 as the ultimate and noblest perfection in things which in turn are ordered to the ultimate uncreated good who is God.

65. Aquinas, *Summa contra Gentiles* 3.112.

66. Aquinas, *Summa theologiae* 1.65.2. The interactive order of all things created by God is the greatest perfection and the most beautiful attribute of creation because it reflects the goodness and wisdom of God,

Aquinas wrote in *Compendium theologiae* 102. Also see *Summa contra Gentiles* 2.42; and *Summa theologiae* 1.2.3, 1.4.2, and 1.13.2.

67. For example, see Aquinas, *Summa theologiae* 1/2.109.3 and 2/2.26.3.

68. Ibid. 1.60.5; see further 2/2.26.3 ad 2.

69. Ibid. 2/2.26.3; he pointed specifically to citizens who suffer losses to their own property and themselves personally for the sake of the common good of their community.

70. Ibid. 1.60.5 ads 3–5; see further 2/2.26.3.

71. Aquinas, *Summa contra Gentiles* 3.24. Also see *Summa theologiae* 1.57.2.

72. Aquinas, *Summa theologiae* 1/2.19.10; his understanding of what is right is based ultimately on an action's being directed toward finality in God.

73. Ibid. 1.22.2. Also see *Summa contra Gentiles* 3.112–13 and *De veritate* 1.5.6–7. According to Aquinas, God's special care is needed for individual humans who have the capacity to think about how to act and choose to act, capacities that humans often misuse. This special divine care for individual humans contrasts with God's general care for other species through natural laws embedded in the physical world because nonhuman creatures do not have intellectual capabilities or free will with which to deviate from God's intentions. God's care for individual humans and other species should be considered in relation to Aquinas's teaching in *Summa contra Gentiles* 3.64 that among God's creation God cares most for the order of all things that constitute the universe.

74. Aquinas, *De veritate* 24.11; see further 27.5.

75. This follows Aquinas's rationale that God governs all things to their end through God's eternal law, which God imposed on the universe in the form of natural law; see, for example, *Summa theologiae* 1/2.91.1, 93.1–5, and *De veritate* 5.1.6. On his thinking about rational creatures who are ruled by eternal law and are rulers of themselves to whom God gives grace to seek their ultimate end, see *Summa theologiae* 1/2.109.1 and *Summa contra Gentiles* 3.1.

76. Aquinas, *Summa theologiae* 1/2.110.1.

77. See, for example, Aquinas, *Summa theologiae* 1.111.2 and *De veritate* 27.5. As Jacques Maritain explained in *The Person and the Common Good*, trans. John J. Fitzgerald (New York: Charles Scribner's Sons, 1947), pp. 7–10, when commenting on *Summa theologiae* 2/2.3.2 ad 2, before humans are "related to the immanent common good of the universe, they are related to an infinitely greater good — the separated common Good, the divine transcendent Whole."

78. Aquinas, *Summa theologiae* 1.11.3; see further 1/2.19.10 on how the common good benefits all constituents of the universe. Also see *Summa contra Gentiles* 1.70, 2.41, 3.69.

79. Aquinas, *Summa theologiae* 1/2.9.1.

80. For example, Aquinas, *De potentia Dei* 4.2 ad 29.

81. Aquinas, *De veritate* 5.2.

82. Aquinas, *Summa theologiae* 1.11.3.

83. Joseph Legrand, *L'univers et l'homme dans la philosophie de Saint Thomas*, 2 vols. (Bruxelles: L'Édition Universelle, 1946), 1, 40.

84. Aquinas, *Compendium theologiae* 124.

85. Ibid.

86. Aquinas, *Summa theologiae* 1.65.2.

87. Ibid.

88. William C. French, "Catholicism and the Common Good of the Biosphere," in *An Ecology of the Spirit: Religious Reflection and Environmental Consciousness,* ed. Michael H. Barnes (Lanham, Md.: University Press of America, 1994), 177–94, at 192. While French sees this organizing principle as a promising response to our contemporary ecological morass, he finds it often "overwhelmed" by another organizing principle, which he describes as "the absolute superiority of rational human life over all lesser creatures," a premise for which he sees little room in theological ethics today. However, he does not factor into his evaluation the severe restrictions Aquinas places on how humans function in relation to other creatures because of their mutual relationship to God. See also Robert P. George, "Natural Law, the Common Good, and American Politics," in *The Battle for the Catholic Mind: Catholic Faith and Catholic Intellect in the Work of the Fellowship of Catholic Scholars, 1978–95,* ed. William E. May and Kenneth D. Whitehead (South Bend, Ind.: St. Augustine, 2001), 308–21; and Brian J. Benestad, "How the Catholic Church Serves the Common Good," in *The Battle for the Catholic Mind,* 443–65.

89. Merle Longwood, "The Common Good: An Ethical Framework for Evaluating Environmental Issues," *Theological Studies* 34 (1973): 468–80, at 479–80. I concur with Longwood's astute conclusion: "Our conception of the common good must obviously include the whole biotic community, since the quality and health of human life is integrally tied to the quality and health of the lives of all the other members of the biosphere. There is, after all, only one ecology, not a human ecology on the one hand and a subhuman ecology on the other."

90. Sallie McFague, *The Body of God: An Ecological Theology* (Minneapolis: Fortress, 1993), 165.

91. IPCC, *Climate Change 2007: Summary Report, Summary for Policy Makers,* Working Group III, 13.2.

92. I am completing this essay as representatives of the nations of the world prepare to congregate in Copenhagen for the United Nations Conference on Climate Change in December 2009. While the news is bleak for reaching an international agreement on mitigating strategies and substantive limits on greenhouse gas emissions in December, there is considerable hope for at least establishing a framework for an agreement to be negotiated in the near future. IPCC, *Climate Change 2007: Synthesis Report,* 62 and 68.

93. In *De veritate* 24.11 and 27.5, Aquinas explained that God offers grace to humans to enable their cooperation with God's intention that they seek the temporal good in this life while aiming for eternal happiness. Aquinas used various versions of *cooperator* to convey three other distinct but related types of cooperation: (1) Creatures cooperate by acting or being acted upon according to their God-given natures for their individual and common good in conformity with the orderly world God created and sustains in existence (e.g., *Summa theologiae* 1.61.3, 111.2, 1/2.9.1 and 19.10, *De veritate* 9.2 and 27.5, *Compendium theologiae* 124, and *Summa contra Gentiles* 1.70, 3.21, and 3.69–70); (2) living creatures cooperate with God, their primary cause for existing, by acting as secondary agents on other creatures to carry out God's plan for the universe (e.g., *Summa theologiae* 1.105.5); and, (3) God both operates on and cooperates with humans for their temporal and eternal good (e.g., *De veritate* 27.5 and *Summa theologiae* 1.105.4–5).

94. IPCC, *Climate Change 2007: Synthesis Report,* 56.

95. IPCC's Working Group III focuses on promising mitigation strategies in its extensive detailed report. See IPCC, *Climate Change 2007: Mitigation of Climate Change,* ed. B. Metz, O. R. Davidson, P. R. Bosch, R. Dave, L. A. Meyer (Cambridge: Cambridge University Press, 2007).

FIVE

Theology and Sustainable Economics

Daniel K. Finn

I WOULD LIKE TO BEGIN with two vignettes that depict our current situation, though from quite different perspectives.

The first concerns two villages in the Swiss Alps, not far from the Italian border. Catholic parishioners there have recently asked for permission of the church to change a prayer they have been saying since the year 1678. Since that day Catholics in the small towns of Fiesch and Fieschertal have been praying that God would spare their villages from being engulfed by the nearby Aletsch Glacier. This glacier, the largest in Europe, had been growing for centuries and residents there were vividly aware of being subject to natural forces over which no earthly power could prevail. For 331 years, they sought God's protection from the encroaching ice. However, the glacier peaked in size in about 1860 and has shrunk back more than a mile in the last few decades. So now Catholics there want to change their prayer and pray for an end to global warming.[1]

The second story is one told by Herman Daly, perhaps the best known environmental economist in the United States. It describes an event from his six years as chief environmental economist at the World Bank.[2] He was hired by the World Bank to bring a greater environmental sophistication to bank analysis, but his immediate superior, Chief Economist Lawrence Summers, was not so convinced of the goal. In contributing a section to the World Bank's annual *World Development Report*, Daly and his colleagues presented not only written analysis but also a graphical depiction of the world economy placed within a rectangle labeled as the planet's biosphere. The intention, of course, was to remind the reader that although conversation about economic life is absolutely essential, we should never forget that every economic action occurs within the limits of the natural world.

Daly was a bit surprised to receive back their proposal with edits from Summers that included instructions to remove the box around the diagram and simply depict only the economy in this graphic, on the argument that this was what the conversation was about. After some internal discussion as to how best to handle this, Daly sent back the next draft, leaving the graphical depiction of the economy within an unlabeled rectangle. This would leave at least a subtle indication that the economy exists within a context. Daly did not see the result until the final report was published, but there he found his graphical depiction of the economy — without the rectangle.

These vignettes summarize well one of the major problems that we face in attempting to address long-term economic sustainability in our culture. What is required is a shift of consciousness from the way we have thought about things not just in recent years but for a very long time. The simple fact is that for nearly all of human history, there was no concern — no need for concern — about global catastrophes caused by human activity. And the discipline of economics itself was born in a world where global environmental catastrophe was not an issue. This has changed and both economics and conventional wisdom now need to change as well.

What I would like to offer in the essay is a framework for thinking about the four problems that every economy faces and an examination of some insights from the Christian theological tradition that can contribute to our resolution of those problems.

The Four Problems of Economic Life

Classically, economists have often talked about the problems that every economy has to find a way to resolve, no matter whether it's through a free market or through some kind of centralized economic command and control. In a well-known work from the 1920s, economist Frank H. Knight identified two general categories of problems. The first category included concerns about what is to be produced, how it should be produced, how much of production goes to immediate consumption and how much to investment, and how to adjust consumption when in the short run production is greater or less than usual. The second sort of problem every economy must address is what he called "the function of distribution," the determination of who gets the goods and services that are produced.[3] Other economists have enumerated a slightly different list of problems, but in general the problems have been identified as what to produce, how to produce it, and to whom that production should go. I would argue, however, that this standard economic approach overlooks two of the critically important problems that every economy has to solve, and thus I would propose that there are four large problems that every economy must address and that any economy may do better or worse at resolving.

The first problem is quite rightly what economists refer to as "allocation." Allocation is the process that gets things made. There are many productive resources in the world, including labor, natural resources, physical capital, and even financial wealth. And these productive resources can be employed in a myriad of different ways. The decisions encompassed by allocation include: which kinds of goods and services will be produced, how much of each good and service will be produced, and how the various productive resources will be combined to produce any one of them. All these decisions are at the core of what both economists and most of the rest of the world think of as "economic" processes. And markets are very good at resolving these questions, though by no means are they perfect.

The great strength of markets is that market prices convey information about how hard it is to have access to various productive inputs and final products, as well as about degree of interest consumers have in those final products. As Charles Lindblom has put it, the market provides coordination without a coordinator.[4] But there are two important ways in which markets fail to allocate resources adequately. The first is that markets are responsive only to those with money enough to buy those final goods and services. Those without sufficient funds don't get a say as to what will be produced. Second, markets would produce (or produce too much of) certain goods and services that are widely considered destructive and would fail to produce (or to produce too little of) certain goods and services that are widely considered to be essential. As Pope John Paul II put it, markets are efficient in utilizing resources and responding to needs, but "this is true only for those needs which are solvent, insofar as they are endowed with purchasing power, and for those resources which are marketable, insofar as they are capable of obtaining a satisfactory price."[5]

Similarly, every nation has laws that forbid the sale of certain kinds of things, whether children, or votes, or shoulder-mounted rocket launchers. Markets would generate such exchanges unless we prevent them. There needs to be a debate about what prohibitions ought to exist, but it's clear that no economy in history has ever existed without the prohibition against the production and sale of certain goods and services considered sufficiently abusive. Similarly, markets on their own will not generate (or will generate too few of) certain goods of social life which no one individual may have an interest to produce but which are essential for an orderly existence, including things from national defense to housing for the homeless to the court system, etc.

The second problem facing every economy is one that economists have also identified: distribution. Simply producing all those products and services isn't enough; one still needs a mechanism for deciding who is to get which of them. Again, there are wide gaps between the moral perspectives of different groups in society, but almost everyone agrees that those who are unable to support themselves deserve the support necessary for a decent life. Some have gone so far as to hope this could be done simply by private, nongovernmental efforts, but such support has never been adequately undertaken in those ways. In fact, the largest religious social service providers in the United States, such as Catholic Charities, Lutheran Social Services, etc., have long received major portions of their budget through government funding. Thus, every economy needs to resolve this problem of distribution and, of course, fundamental moral values from religious traditions are a critical part of the resolution.

The third problem of economic life, one that is the focus of this conference, is the problem of scale. For most of the history of the world there have not been any examples of large-scale environmental disasters caused by humans. There have, however, been local environmental disasters. For example, the abrupt abandonment of the cliff-dwellings in what is now Mesa Verde National Park in southwest Colorado about the year 1200 seems to have been caused by an overstress on the local environment.[6] And lest we think that industrial pollution problems are new, it is instructive to note a report in the *London Times* in January 1812, nearly two hundred years ago, describing that miasma of fog and coal smoke that regularly filled the air and lungs of London. Describing the previous day, the *Times* report said "it was impossible to read or write at a window without artificial light. Persons in the street could scarcely be seen in the forenoon at two yards distance."[7] Still, prior to the industrial age, our ecological footprint was neither large enough nor heavy enough to make much of a global impression.

Markets are notoriously incompetent in recognizing problems of scale when they arise. The fundamental reason for this, of course, is that market transactions are usually one-to-one transactions. You make an offer and I accept or reject; I make an offer and you accept or reject. The market by itself does not include third-party effects and if there are no mechanisms — legal or cultural — that press us to take into consideration those effects, people will often continue their transactions ignoring those effects on others. As Herman Daly and John Cobb have argued in language familiar to economists, determining the appropriate scale for the economy within the biosphere is a "distinct optimization problem," a problem that cannot be subsumed under the usual economic notion of achieving an allocative optimum.[8]

The twentieth century saw the first general awareness that the sum total of all human economic activity is now quite capable of overwhelming the capacity of the planet to absorb its waste products and provide sufficient natural resources for all of the planet's people to replicate the standard of living typical of citizens in the industrialized world. As with the first two problems (i.e., allocation and distribution), there are many moral issues in this consideration of scale, including how we should assess the interests of generations yet unborn. With a long-term perspective like Christianity has, we can clearly see resources within the tradition for thinking through this problem. We will return to this theme.

The fourth problem of economic life is one largely ignored by most economists: the quality of economic relationships. Economic analysis tends to take for granted that people want to enter into economic transactions. It does not spend much time on the kind of personal virtues and cultural expectations that improve or harm the effectiveness of economic processes. Fundamentally, the success of an economy depends upon the well-being that the economy generates for the people of that society. Psychological studies have clearly shown that human well-being arises not simply from having an adequate income but even more fundamentally from one's relationships, though an adequate income plays an essential part in sustaining those relationships. Thus if we could not trust that our co-workers will respect us and will not steal from us, the quality of our lives together would be diminished. In fact, large corporations spend immense amounts of money developing a "corporate culture," an explicit attempt to foster trust and respect between individuals and departments within the same firm. Rebecca Blank has argued, "Economic institutions also shape norms and political practices."[9] After all, most people spend more hours at their job than anywhere else other than at home. For this reason the impact of the relationships in economic life extend far beyond its ordinary purview. It can improve or weaken what has come to be called the "social capital" of a society, just as important a resource as the natural world for constructing a humane life together.[10] Thus, whether adverted to explicitly or not, the quality of economic relationships is another problem that every economy faces.

The Christian Tradition and Economic Life

There are many ways to approach the question of sustainable economic life within the Christian tradition. I will here focus on just one of those ways, namely, the Christian doctrine of creation.[11] In order to prevent any misunderstanding, let me recall that the fundamental theological view of this doctrine is quite different from the belief in "creationism," which is a belief on the part of fundamentalist Christians that the Bible is scientifically accurate and thus modern science must be erroneous. The Catholic Church and the mainline Protestant churches reject creationism since God is quite capable of creating the world through natural processes over the last 14 billion years.

The creation stories of Genesis are well known and in the interest of time I will refer here only to two general principles that Christian theology has drawn from this Hebraic view of God's creation which we inherit. These are that creation is good and that creation is a gift.

The first creation account in Genesis reports that after each day of creation, God "saw that it was good." That is, the material world, in all its complexity and beauty, is understood from a religious point of view as good, not bad and not even simply neutral, but good. The Christian's relationship with the material world is part of that goodness, and Christians do not understand their spiritual well-being as somehow defined separate from or in rejection of the material world. Some religious perspectives in the world understand the ideal spiritual situation as one where one escapes the material world and retreats as much as possible to a purely spiritual place where the religiously important can occur. Christians have rejected this point of view. As Jame Schaefer has put in her very helpful volume *Theological Foundations for Environmental Ethics,* "thinking about the physical world's goodness is deeply embedded in patristic and medieval texts by some of Christianity's most eminent theologians, including Augustine of Hippo, John Chrysostom, and Thomas Aquinas."[12] John Chrysostom, for example, argued that his listeners should "shun like a lunatic" anyone who did not agree with God's view about the world's goodness. It was "arrogant folly" for anyone to dispute the goodness of the created world.[13]

I teach at a university sponsored by a large Benedictine monastery, and it is a cultural fact that many people today think of monasteries as places where monks go to "escape from the world," to reject the material world, and to do something purely spiritual. This, however, is a fundamental misunderstanding of what has occurred in monasticism over the last fifteen hundred years. After the conversion of the Roman emperor Constantine in the early fourth century, it became socially advantageous to be a Christian, and thus the faith of many believers was not particularly strong. Christian monasticism began as a move away from the cities to establish communities, but the reason was not to reject the material world but to reject a watered-down life of faith. As the Rule of Benedict indicates, a careful treatment of tools, pots, pans, and other implements of the monastery are mandated, and even the most menial kinds of work are recognized as religiously important. To take but one example, the Rule of Benedict calls for a peculiar event to occur at the first gathering for prayer ("Lauds") each Sunday morning, the first day of the week. Benedict says that those monks who have worked in the kitchen the previous week as well

as those scheduled to begin this week's kitchen service are to come
before the monks at Morning Prayer and the community is to pray
for and with them.[14] One might think that in a community of men,
where there were no women to rely on for the menial job of clean-
ing those dirty pots and pans, we might detect an attitude that this
sort of work is nasty but unavoidable. Instead, Benedict insists that
like all kinds of work, it is dignified and worthy of the most fundamental respect, so fundamental that on the first occasion of prayer
on the morning of the first day of the week those on kitchen duty
receive the prayer and respect of all.

This is only one brief example of how Christian theology has
consistently understood the material world as good and that this
goodness is not something simply created by human action but is
a divine creation, a goodness that God recognized at the moment
of creation. If we humans are to respect the material world as God
respects it, we must recognize its role in creation. Thus we hear the
psalmist say:

> Praise the LORD from the earth, you great sea creatures
>   and all ocean depths,
> lightning and hail, snow and clouds, stormy winds that
>   do his bidding,
> you mountains and all hills, fruit trees and all cedars,
> wild animals and all cattle, small creatures and flying
>   birds,
> kings of the earth and all nations, you princes and all
>   rulers on earth,
> young men and maidens, old men and children.
> Let them praise the name of the LORD, for his name
>   alone is exalted;
> his splendor is above the earth and the heavens.
>   Psalm 148:7–13

Nature has integrity separate from human well-being and can both
reflect and praise the glory of God.

The second major theme arising out of the Christian doctrine
of creation is that the world around us is a gift. Most vividly in
Israelite history, God brought the Israelites out of slavery in Egypt
and established them in their own land, one flowing with milk and
honey. Thus, in Christian faith we are not simply finding ourselves

on this planet as a result of a meaningless stochastic process in some kind of cosmic lottery. Instead, we understand the material world as a gift from God, one the Israelites saw clearly as part of the covenant with the Lord, a mutual binding of God and people in which there were intricate rules for how this gift is to be used and treated.

Thus, for example, the Torah included economic laws that restricted what owners could do with their property. According to the Hebrew Scriptures, if I own a field of grain I am not to harvest the corners of the field but should leave it there for the widow, the orphan, and the resident alien. These groups, of course, are what today we would call "the poor" in ancient Israel. Similar laws related to the sabbatical and jubilee years indicate a fundamental concern in ancient Israel for sustaining even the weakest among us, and to ensure that that sustenance carries on over the long run.

We should step back here and make a note about method in Christian theology. It is a simple fact that all human speech is contextual, every sentence spoken, every word uttered, has meaning only because of the cultural and linguistic context in which it occurs, and thus for someone in this audience today to stand up and to begin to speak in Urdu, a language used in much of India, would likely leave the rest of us completely baffled. Words, their meanings, and all human intellectual activity are contextual. It's important to note the connection between this insight and the earlier observation that prior to the modern world there was no experience of widespread environmental problems caused by human action. That is, environmental damage was not a problem that Hebrew and early Christian thinkers reflected upon, just as we will search in vain for a treatment of nuclear weapons or the Internet in these ancient texts. However, human thought and theology itself is a flexible instrument, and thus when new problems arise we are often able to find resources for treating those problems even in texts that did not have those problems explicitly in mind.

Thus today we are experiencing a growth of interest in those resources of the Christian tradition that are available for addressing contemporary environmental problems. We have already seen that the psalmist's belief that the material world gives glory to God indicates that nature has an integrity separate from our own well-being and that it is part of God's plan that we respect that integrity even while we depend upon and use nature for our daily needs. Thus today we can understand that the obligations of property ownership identified in the Bible should apply not just to our limiting our own ownership in regard to sharing our goods with the poor, but also limiting our ownership claims in respect for the goodness and integrity of nature.

Thus Christian theology today cautions us that whatever system of property ownership we might employ, we must insist that the ownership be limited so that the two dimensions of sustainable economic life will be respected. The first is sustaining the lives of all persons, not just those who are well-to-do. This, of course, indicts not just those who make more than, say, $100,000 a year, but all of us, since on a world scale we are among the wealthy. Second, Christian theology insists that we attend to the sustenance of nature itself over the long term. Of course, this goal conflicts with human flourishing if we define human flourishing as having whatever we want. And sorting out those potential conflicts between respect for the integrity of nature and human flourishing itself is an involved process.

Catholic social thought provides a fundamental comprehensive notion that is very helpful in thinking through trade-offs: the common good. There are many definitions of the common good available today and the one that is most popular is also fatally flawed. Most people think of the common good as the sum total of the good experienced by all individuals in society and think of the good experienced by each individual as the total of good experiences in life minus bad experiences in life. The fundamental problem with this view of the common good is that a small proportion of the population can live in terrible deprivation and yet this can be offset by the great prosperity of others so that it looks on average like the society as a whole is doing pretty well.

A far more adequate explanation of the common good is provided by Virgil Michel, a Benedictine monk at St. John's in Collegeville, who died in 1938. Following good Thomistic tradition, Virgil Michel finds the common good as having two dimensions.[15] The first is the "common conditions of social life." Here Michel anticipates the later definition of the common good used both in *Mater et Magistra* and the document of the Second Vatican Council *Gaudium et Spes:* "the sum total of conditions of social living, whereby persons are enabled more fully and readily to achieve their own perfection."[16] These common conditions include both the experience of peace, security, truth, and beauty, and those institutional structures, organizations, and frameworks that we all depend on and that none of us can create on our own. We need things like the police and courts, an educational system, occupational opportunity, museums, parks, and roads, and a large number of other elements that make for a good life for each of us as individuals.

The second dimension is "the attainment of the good life by all, at least to a minimum degree." Here we recognize that every individual must be included in the common good and that even the poorest person should have an experience of the good life to a minimum degree, so that their basic needs are met and they are able to live, as Pope Leo XIII once put it, "in reasonable and frugal comfort."[17]

Today, recognized among the elements necessary for those common conditions of social life are the integrity of nature and the ongoing capacity of our planet to provide resources for future generations and to receive the wastes of human life. These environmental concerns were by no means clear to scholars a hundred years ago, but today it is clear that common-good analysis must include not simply the well-being of persons but also the well-being of nature itself.

Revisiting the Four Problems of Economic Life

If we now return to the four problems that every economy must face, employing the insights of Christian theology, we can see the ways in which our theological perspective can provide helpful insight into the resolution of these problems. We should note here that there will usually be a gap between the general principles that Christians should be able to agree upon and concrete policy decisions, about which Christians and others of goodwill may rightly disagree. This is sometimes frustrating for people because, of course, we would all like a very specific answer. However Christianity itself and certainly Catholicism within it, has a worldwide perspective and the creation of policy is always dependent upon the particular need at the time and the particular history of that nation. Thus the popes have always said that the church itself does not have a particular economic plan to offer. As Pope John Paul II put it, "The Church has no models to present; models that are real and truly effective can only arise within the framework of different historical situations, through the efforts of all those who responsibly confront concrete problems in all their social, economic, political and cultural aspects, as these interact with one another."[18] Nonetheless, the general principles do indeed limit the number of policy options that are available, and such principles actually rule out of bounds some of the policy proposals espoused by some Christians even today.

If we turn to the problem of allocation, one of the ways of understanding the intervention of moral concerns in the allocation process is to say that we must prevent uneconomic growth.[19] This phrase, coined by Herman Daly, points to the problem that our allocation process may produce products and pollution byproducts that we do not want and often will not produce products and services that are badly needed. To take one current economic example, there is a growing awareness that we have underinvested in alternative forms of energy production, and overinvested in carbon-based energy, largely because we have ignored the external cost of the escape of carbon dioxide into the atmosphere.

Economists have a perceptive analysis of such "externalities," that is, effects on third parties that the two contracting parties do not and sometimes cannot take into consideration. Externalities, these third-party effects, can be either positive or negative. We are most familiar with the negative externalities of pollution and understand that the polluting factory will have to be required to change its ways because market forces alone are not going to make it happen. But standing back let us think about something that has a positive externality, something like the very attractive lawns around that corporate headquarters you drive by on your way to work. You get to enjoy what looks like a public park without having to spend any of your money to help create it. The corporation generates this positive externality for those in the area.

Other more important positive externalities have brought about changes in public policy. When your children become better educated, I am better off, because in a democracy your children will participate in electing public officials. And when your children get vaccinated, my children can be healthier, since with fewer classmates who are likely to be ill, my children are less likely to be ill as well. Thus, both education and vaccination have positive externalities and, taking the latter example, if we left it to the market to decide how much vaccination would occur, each parent would tend to decide on vaccinating their children based on (1) the amount of good they see will be caused by the vaccination for their own family and (2) the cost of any particular vaccination. Economists argue that vaccinations are underproduced in the market because the family deciding to buy vaccinations cannot capture any advantages such vaccinations will give to other families. This is the standard economic justification for the public subsidy of vaccinations and education and other processes where there are significant positive externalities.

Clearly the same issue applies today with regard to experimentation and development of alternative energy sources and a large number of alternative production processes. Because these more benign ways to produce energy and products will benefit not just the persons producing and consuming a product but also all of us, and since effective new technologies can be replicated by others, there is a strong economic case for the public subsidy of those activities. Similarly, the same economic logic calls for greater penalties imposed on those processes that produce harm to the environment, and thus some form of carbon tax would be an optimal economic solution for moving from our current unsustainable energy future into a different one for our children.

Distribution, the second problem of economic life, tends to be focused on the inability of some in our economy to support themselves, whether because they are too old, too young, incapacitated, or simply unable to find work. A separate category, which is becoming better and better known, is often referred to as "environmental justice." It is concerned with sustainability issues in terms of their effect on the poor. Time and again environmentally damaging facilities from industrial smokestacks to toxic waste dumps have been located where they affect the lives of the poor more than the wealthy, who live "upstream," both geographically and culturally. This occurs both within our communities in the industrialized world and between communities the world over. But even separate from this process, it is also true that poverty itself can be very hard on the environment. About three-quarters of all the wood harvested

in Asia is used for fuel and in Africa the number is over 90 percent. Take for example the needs of the poor in many arid regions
of Africa to simply cook their food each evening. When there are
no other alternative fuels, the harvest of wood is intense and in
many regions of Africa the major cause of deforestation is the very
poverty of the poor, who have no other choices but to cut down
nearby forests to survive. Thus there is a close and important connection between distributive justice and sustainable economic life.
Much more work needs to be done here, both in terms of public
awareness and careful social scientific analysis of the problem and
its solutions.

The third problem facing every economy is that of scale, and here
reside the most fundamental issues of sustainable economic life. I
will not attempt to summarize here the many related environmental issues but it remains critically important that we recognize the
limitations of markets in grasping and dealing with the problem of
scale. The issue here as indicated earlier is not that markets are of no
help in addressing scale but rather that the fundamental one-to-one
interaction that occurs in a market produces few internal incentives
for the contracting parties to worry about the problem of scale. To
get a bit of perspective on the problem of scale in environmental
issues it is helpful to note that our current economic crisis arises in
some large part from the problem of scale in the financial world and
the difficulties that occurred because, in common parlance, there
were firms that were "too big to fail." That is, just as the physical
environment is unable to handle the scale of environmental impact
without eventual cataclysmic results, so too our financial system
has gotten so large and the problems of risk assessment so complex
that when one of the dominoes begins to fall many others fall at
the same time in a way that even the experts cannot predict. And
just as tighter regulation of derivatives and other exotic financial
instruments is required (along with a number of other changes), so
there can be a resolution of the environmental problems we face
only if we think realistically about the limitations of markets.

And yet to be clear, once the communal decision is made to intervene in markets to create a sustainable economic future, there are
market mechanisms that may well be very helpful. Thus carbon
taxes and cap and trade systems, both good market-based options,
are examples of employing some of the strengths of markets to solve

problems in a regulated environment that are caused by unregulated markets in the first place.

The fourth problem is the quality of economic relationships. Just as the problem of scale tends to focus our attention on our relationship with the natural environment, so this fourth problem focuses our attention on human persons. There is, however, a strong relationship among the various functions of care: persons who care about others often exercise a set of virtues quite similar to those necessary in caring for the natural world. Both attempt a kind of integrity of life that is too easily set aside if narrow economic goals of wealth creation dominate human consciousness. That is, participation in economic life ought to maintain our moral integrity even while we take on roles on Monday morning different from those we have on the weekend. It is a fundamental requirement of Catholic social thought that the goal we have for ourselves is not simply to become wealthier or happier, but rather the goal is "integral human development." After all, the full title of Benedict XVI's most recent encyclical is *On Integral Human Development in Charity and Truth*.

Conclusion

I would conclude this all too brief treatment of theology and sustainable economics with a few questions for us to wrestle with. The first concerns the difficulty of the contextual character of theological reflection. What challenges do you see in broadening the church's understanding of human economic life to include concerns about the environment that were not addressed in earlier eras, largely because the problems of the environment were not obvious at that time? Second, how do you understand the trade-off between care for persons and care for nature? On the one hand, the Christian tradition has always placed human dignity and concern for persons as the highest earthly goal, and yet today we realize that that concern cannot occur and humans cannot flourish without a sustainable planet on which to live. Some have argued that nature itself has rights, while others have said only humans have rights but that the charge to humans in Genesis to oversee God's creation includes a vibrant obligation to act as responsible stewards. Third and last, what trade-offs would you be willing to experience in your own life? What parts of your current definition of well-being would you be willing to give up for there to be a more sustainable future for our lives together?

These are not easy questions but are critically important if we are to think through creatively, responsibly, and faithfully, the relation of God, creation, and the environmental crisis.

Notes

1. "In Brief," *The Tablet,* August 15, 2009, 30.

2. Oral conversation, October 26, 1999.

3. Frank H. Knight, *The Economic Organization* (New York: Augustus M. Kelley, 1967), 3–15. Knight's essay was originally written in the 1920s though not published until 1951.

4. Charles E. Lindblom, *The Market System: What It Is, How It Works, and What to Make of It* (New Haven, Conn.: Yale University Press, 2001), 23.

5. John Paul II, *Centesimus Annus,* para. 34.

6. Elenor H. Ayer, *The Anasazi* (New York: Walker and Company, 1993), 60–63; William M. Ferguson, *The Anasazi of Mesa Verde and the Four Corners* (Boulder: University Press of Colorado, 1996), 99–100, 114.

7. *The Times,* January 11, 1812, quoted in Barbara Freese, *Coal: A Human History* (Cambridge, Mass.: Perseus Books, 2003), 27.

8. Herman E. Daly and John B. Cobb Jr., *For the Common Good: Redefining Economy toward Community, the Environment, and a Sustainable Future* (Boston: Beacon Press, 1989), 145.

9. Rebecca M. Blank and William McGurn, *Is the Market Moral? A Dialogue on Religion, Economics and Justice* (Washington, D.C.: Brookings Institution Press, 2004), 97.

10. For further information on social capital see Ismail Serageldin and Christiaan Grootaert, *Defining Social Capital: An Integrating View* (Washington, D.C.: World Bank, 1997), 47, and John Coleman, S.J., "Wealth Creation, Social Virtues and Sociality: Social Capital's Role in Creating and Sustaining Wealth," *True Wealth of Nations* (New York: Oxford University Press, 2010).

11. For a Christian perspective that rejects creation as an adequate starting point for an environmental theology, see Odil Hannes Steck, *World and Environment,* Biblical Encounters Series (Nashville: Abingdon, 1978).

12. Jame Schaefer, *Theological Foundations for Environmental Ethics: Reconstructing Patristic and Medieval Concepts* (Washington, D.C.: Georgetown University Press, 2009).

13. John Chrysostom, *Homilies on Genesis*, 10.13, 137, cited in Schaefer, *Theological Foundations for Environmental Ethics*, 25.

14. Rule of St. Benedict, Chap. XXXV.

15. Virgil Michel, O.S.B., "The Common Good," in *Christian Social Reconstruction* (Milwaukee: Bruce Publishing Company, 1937), 120–32.

16. *Mater et Magistra* 65; *Gaudium et Spes* 26.

17. Pope Leo XIII, *Rerum Novarum* para 34.

18. *Centesimus Annus* 43.

19. Herman Daly, "Uneconomic Growth: In Theory, in Fact, in History, and in Relation to Globalization," in Herman Daly and Edward Elgar, *Ecological Economics and the Ecology of Economics: Essays in Criticism* (Cheltenham, UK: Edward Elgar, 1999).

SIX

Another Call to Action

CATHOLICS AND THE CHALLENGE
OF CLIMATE CHANGE

David J. O'Brien

A T THE END of a conference, or a book of essays, comes the inevitable question about action. "What Is to Be Done?" was the title of Lenin's famous manifesto translating Karl Marx's frustratingly philosophical analysis of capitalism into a program of practical action, with terrible consequences. But lest we become cynical, every exposé of a social problem requires a response. We older Catholics of Catholic Action days learned that lesson through this formula (later given papal blessing by Pope Paul VI): observe, judge, act. Leo XIII got this started in *Rerum Novarum* in 1891 when he took an unblinking look at industrial society, assessed its practices in light of traditional Christian teachings, and suggested an outline of action: living wages, labor unions, social legislation. Later Pope John XXIII, after the Cuban Missile Crisis of 1962, invited the world family to take the road away from war by affirming human rights and constructing institutions appropriate to the goal of *Pacem in Terris,* peace on earth.

Now, in a conference in Kansas City, and in this book, we have joined other Catholics, from the Vatican to alert parishes, community gardens and experimental agrarian communities, in facing up to hard facts about our environment, reflecting on those facts in light of the Gospel and church teaching, and considering the classic question of what do we do now. It is an important step, as those old Catholic Action leaders knew. In its absence, after yet another exercise in consciousness-raising, we risk ending the conversation with the feeling expressed by a lay friend of mine years ago when he referred to our group's church-basement presentations on violence as the "ain't it awful" approach to Christianity. We feel really bad as we leave the hall, but let's not miss lunch!

Mobilizing the Catholic Community

So what are we to do? Inviting me to join this project editor Richard Miller pushed that envelope, suggesting a title that included words about "mobilizing Catholics" for action on the environment. His words reminded me of an incident almost forty years ago when I participated in an ecumenical workshop on faith and politics at the Johnson Foundation's Wingspread Center in Wisconsin. Also attending was a young evangelical scholar who shared my interest in what was then called "the Christian left," he as a participant in the new Sojourners community, I through friendships with Catholic Workers that had nurtured my early scholarly career and transformed my own "faith and politics." As one day's discussion ended, my evangelical colleague and I were invited to visit the room of a slightly older and very well known Lutheran pastor, then a leader of the Christian left as a co-founder of Clergy and Laity Concerned about the War in Vietnam. This handsome, eloquent fellow told us that together we could change the world. With his help we could unite Catholics and evangelicals in a broad political movement to back the civil rights movement, oppose the Vietnam War, and overcome poverty, and in the process reshape American political culture. Still somewhat innocent about such matters, I thought that was an excellent idea, but my evangelical friend listened quietly and, when our host paused for a breath, he smiled and said "get behind me, Satan." Some of you will have guessed by now that our host that evening, the late Richard Neuhaus, succeeded, years later, as a Catholic priest, in pulling off that ecumenical coalition and for a moment at least changing American politics, but from a different angle from that of Sojourners and the Catholic Worker.

So mobilizing all those American Catholics for a public purpose is an idea that has intrigued reformers for a long time. Early in the last century there was a promising American Federation of Catholic Societies composed of ethnic, benevolent, and fraternal organizations hoping to work together to defend the church and protect its interests. About the same time Monsignor John A. Ryan, the leader of Catholic social action for half a century, tried to mobilize Catholic clergy and laity to support progressive legislation for social justice. Toward that end he persuaded the bishops to set up a strong social action office within their new national conference established after World War I. In the 1930s he saw at least partial fulfillment of his hopes as Catholic organizations distributed pamphlets about papal social teaching and rallied to the support of the New Deal and the burgeoning labor movement. In those years many also mobilized in response to the demagogic appeals of the radio priest Father Charles E. Coughlin, who campaigned across the country for a third party presidential candidate in 1936. Other lay people rallied to social action groups like the new Catholic Worker movement, the Catholic Rural Life Conference, and the Association of Catholic Trade Unionists.[1]

Social justice was not and is not the only area of projects for Catholic mobilization. Cultural historians describe another "Catholic Front" in the 1930s as newly assertive Catholics saw the Great Depression as an opportunity to promote Catholic alternatives to dominant left-wing ideas in the media, radio, theater, and famously the movies. Later, after World War II, all across the country, Catholics paraded to stadiums, often under Marian banners, to champion America's cause during the Cold War.[2] In the 1960s many Catholics worked hard to build Catholic support for the civil rights movement, the movement to end the war in Vietnam, the war on poverty, and the campaign of California farm workers led by César Chávez. They enjoyed considerable support from church professionals, even from bishops, whose pastoral letters on race, nuclear weapons, and economic justice in the 1980s marked a highpoint of what was coming to be called "public Catholicism."

Those Catholic efforts at peace and social justice, associated with the leadership of Cardinal Joseph Bernardin, were deliberately detached from mass mobilization, in contrast to bishop-led, and surprisingly popular, efforts to mobilize Catholics against abortion. The latter movement had its root in the Catholic cultural front of the 1930s, and in the campaigns against birth control, secularism, and communism in the postwar era. On often divisive social and economic issues the bishops and other church leaders were cautious, but on cultural issues, where they believed basic teachings were at stake, they risked division and adopted moral positions that allowed little compromise. At times they did not hesitate to mobilize Catholics for specific action. I recall parish-based campaigns against relaxing bans on birth control in Massachusetts when I was ten, and as we speak the Catholic bishop of Maine has made support for an upcoming referendum question overturning gay marriage legislation a matter of Catholic orthodoxy and loyalty, complete with pulpit messages, special collections, and participation in rallies and mass mailings. Experience of these campaigns elsewhere, and of Catholic political experience in recent years, suggests that such efforts at Catholic mobilization pose serious pastoral problems, risk internal divisions, and have mixed results in terms of overcoming the moral issues that occasion that mobilization.

As for climate change and other environmental issues, responsible Catholic leaders have already offered us multiple answers to the action question. Papers in this volume have taken full note of the remarkable leadership of so many Catholics on these matters. By this time we have heard about the teaching of the Holy Father and the work of Vatican agencies, and of the clear and forceful statements and calls to action of the U.S. bishops. Reference has been made to the environmental office of the USCCB, to Catholic Relief Services, the Catholic Rural Life Conference, and the Catholic Coalition for Climate Change. Bishop William Skylstad, past president of the USCCB, recently summarized current teaching and offered useful suggestions we should all hear:

> The Catholic Coalition for Climate Change . . . is also launching a practical education and action initiative. Individual Catholics, families, parishes, schools, religious communities, dioceses, and other Catholic organizations are invited to take the St. Francis Pledge and join the Catholic Climate Covenant. The covenant provides concrete ways of responding to Scripture and Catholic teaching, while demonstrating a concern for both the planet and its people. Through a new Web site, video, and ad campaign with outreach to dozens of cooperating national organizations, Catholics are being asked to take the pledge and agree to *pray and reflect* on the duty to care for God's creation and protect the poor and vulnerable; *learn about and educate others* on the moral dimensions

of climate change; *assess our participation* — as individuals
and organizations — in contributing to climate change; *act
to change choices and behaviors* that contribute to climate
change; and *advocate Catholic principles and priorities* in
discussions and in decision-making on climate change, especially as it affects the poor and vulnerable. A new Web site
(*http://usccb.org/sdwp/ejp/climate*) will provide concrete ways
for Catholics to fulfill their pledge.[3]

I have many times helped craft statements like that and worked
with Catholic agencies to have social education and action programs and ideas ready for people, parishes, and schools. In a well
organized and flourishing church there would be little more to say
but go home and get to work: materials would be distributed,
preachers would preach, teachers teach, religious orders would initiate programs, diocesan social action offices would monitor local,
state, and federal legislation, interreligious coalitions would emerge,
and all of our consciences would be well-formed as disciples and
citizens.

But recent experience suggests the need to think a little harder
about our historical experience and how we can best fulfill our
not always integrated responsibilities as disciples and citizens. Part
of the context of that rethinking as Americans is the obvious and
costly absence of organized political support for the common good
and the public interest as distinct from what we all call "special
interests" (at least we call them special interests when they are not
our own). Another part of that context for us, as Catholics, is that
our church is divided on many questions of public responsibility.
Even basic questions of the nature and purpose of the church, and
thus of individual and communal responsibility, are contested, as
recent highly publicized disputes have made very clear. Those divisions will likely hamper any serious effort to build mass Catholic
support for environmental justice. And our institutional resources
are changing: the USCCB has downsized, national offices have
far smaller budgets and staffs, bishops have fewer agencies with
which to forward projects developed in Rome or Washington. Who,
then, has responsibility to take the next steps suggested by Bishop
Skylstad?

Catholic Social Gospel, Social Teaching, and Social Action

It seems to me that we American Catholics have developed three ways of engaging our country's public life. Let's call them Catholic social teaching, Catholic social action, and Catholic social gospel. Taking them in reverse order Catholic social gospel emerges when in response to a social problem we ask, "What would Jesus do?" and then translate Gospel imperative into a directive for action: think of the option for the poor or Christian nonviolence. Catholic social teaching constitutes the community's age-old reflection on trying to live out those Gospel mandates in changing historical circumstances: think of corporate responsibility and just war. And Catholic social action arises when you actually try to do something effective: think of a young war resister accompanying civilians through daily routines in war-torn Iraq in 2006 or you and your friends trying to implement the idea that the poor should be the agents of their own liberation in your hometown.

These three approaches have not always fit well together. For example, after a great talk on the Catholic ethics of war and peace, a young man noted that the speaker had not mentioned Jesus. His talk had used natural law categories of human dignity and the common good in order to engage everyone, Christians and non-Christians alike, in the conversation about a matter of public policy. To take another example, recently, Pope Benedict, reflecting on Gospel terms like "love" and "gift," echoed the appeal of Catholic Worker founder Peter Maurin that we not turn our labor into a commodity. Friends shuddered when I suggested we take up this idea with the local business school. And after all our civic efforts at moral consensus and our ecclesiastical efforts at Gospel fidelity we notice that, in Washington and down the street, power is what matters, and power seems usually to come from money and organization, not from dialogue or prayer. Once we may have relied on elites, kings, or experts, to handle governmental affairs; ordinary people did not have to worry about such matters. But once we understood that we lacked angels in the form of leaders to govern us, we decided we had to govern ourselves. This complicates Catholic political responsibility and raises questions about the appropriate way of responding to the call to action on climate change.

First, let us look at Catholic social teaching, from John Ryan through John Courtney Murray to recent luminaries like J. Bryan Hehir. Ryan championed the living wage, and he and his students actually led the national fight for minimum wage laws. Priests he trained supported trade unions, so did the bishops, and eventually there were labor priests and a network of Catholic labor schools across the country. Ryan, called by a critic "the Right Reverend New Dealer," famously persuaded the bishops to endorse basic social welfare legislation and showed the way to a political strategy in which the church would help lay Catholics form their consciences for carrying out their political responsibilities. You will recognize here the approach later championed by Murray, endorsed by the Vatican Council, and brought to an American climax under the leadership of Cardinal Bernardin. It remains the mainstream approach, reflected in the election guidebook *Faithful Citizenship*, in Bishop Skylstad's words, and in the day-to-day work of the major Catholic agencies charged with social responsibility.

Several items should be noted. First, Catholics have had limited success. They helped win minimum wage laws but not the living wages affirmed by church teaching. They helped establish self-interested unions dedicated to better wages, hours, benefits and working conditions for their members, but not a share of corporate responsibility for labor, as championed by popes or the "economic democracy" affirmed by Ryan. Catholics contributed to bread-and-butter liberal reforms of the New Deal variety, all backed under the heading of distributive justice, but were less effective in achieving full employment, adequate housing, or universal medical care supported by the bishops. Moreover the reliance on distributive justice left Catholic advocates vulnerable to "expanding pie" arguments that asked about the production rather than distribution of wealth. More generally, few Catholics who supported the short-term goals of social justice understood or accepted the long-term goals in which those proposals were embedded.

Second, it should be noted that there has been an absence, in the post–Vatican II era, of a pastoral strategy to implement the vision of the church as a community of conscience respectful of the autonomy of the laity. The pope teaches, we were told, then priests preach, the rest of us learn and form our conscience. Occasionally the clergy, with the help of experts, meet with policy makers to help form the public moral consensus needed for common action. Any effective social activist, from early labor organizers to recent civil rights workers, could have told us that would not work. Historically the Catholic Church in the United States had an effective if sometimes implicit pastoral strategy for dealing with the poor, but never developed an effective strategy for its Americanized middle-class population. For evidence of this claim simply go back and read the closing pastoral sections of the famous letters of the 1980s, one on peace and the other on the economy: they contained no ringing calls to public service or civic action and almost no mention of the role of the laity in carrying out the social mission of the church.

Third, it should be noted that despite all these shortcomings, Catholic social teaching is a comprehensive and rich body of ideas that contains much that is badly needed today: defense of human life and human rights, insistence on shared political responsibility, and perhaps most needed an emphasis on solidarity and the common good. But the process by which these ideas influence public life is far from automatic. If that influence is to be felt it will be the result, and only the result, of deliberate purposeful pastoral action, itself dependent on organized deliberation and mobilization. That work remains to be done.

Similar comments could be made about what I have called the Catholic social gospel. We associate this first of all with those we have thought of as Catholic "radicals" like Dorothy Day and the Catholic Workers, with their commitment to Gospel nonviolence and, in Peter Maurin's words, to creating a society in which it is easier to be good. By the grace of God both sets of ideas, nonviolence and communitarian economics, have found their way into the heart of contemporary Catholic teaching. Moreover, Catholic piety, increasingly evangelical in an American fashion, is in many ways more comfortable with Gospel-based reflection than the careful ethical constructions of most Catholic social thought. Even today, where justice seeking and peacemaking find so much support in formal church statements, the passion for action arises around scriptural ideas of creation, incarnation, and redemption, and the Sermon on the Mount. "What would Jesus do?" almost always trumps "What does the church teach?"

Notice how the social gospel, probably more than Catholic social teaching, ties into our own formation of conscience and, I suspect, into our religious education programs. Notice, too, how this approach can easily become trivialized or sentimentalized, as it often is among our evangelical brothers and sisters. Notice, too, how this approach has lacked an adequate pastoral strategy. Notre Dame's Michal Baxter, the closest we have to a Catholic Worker theologian, taught a course entitled "Faith to Die For" but graduates must have asked what to do for work and family if one was not drawn to Catholic Worker communities. The social gospel gives rise to a politics of witness and "ultimate ends" but is not so helpful when it comes to the policy choices and economic reforms required by such challenges as global warming. It's a long way from fasting and turning down the heat to the cap and trade bill.

If the key word with Catholic social thought is "dialogue," and the key word with the Catholic social gospel is "witness," then the key word with Catholic social and political action has been "organize." Neighborhood parishes and schools, ethnic networks and associations, political machines and trade unions were the vehicles through which millions of working class American Catholics achieved genuine liberation. Thirty years ago veteran Catholic social action leaders drew on that historical experience to create the Catholic Campaign for Human Development, channeling millions of dollars toward grassroots, self-help organizations among the poor. Today the most vigorous social action work among Latinos and new immigrants is often congregation-based community organizing that draws on this rich heritage. American Catholics became pretty good at organizing for power, uniting for the pursuit of group interests, and negotiating the best solutions they could get. This approach is supported by the Gospel teachings about human dignity and church teaching that the poor should be the agents of their own liberation, but it is too democratic and too "political" for most pastors, teachers, and theologians. It remains the least noticed element of the American Catholic social justice heritage.

None of these approaches (i.e., Catholic social teaching, Catholic social gospel, and Catholic social action) came close to mobilizing most Catholics, much less winning pieces of the Kingdom of God, but together they constitute a multipronged American Catholic tradition that fostered an amazing array of institutions for education, medical care, and social services. They helped line Catholics up,

sometimes reluctantly, behind many of the changes that democra-
tized American life, like labor unions and social security. Indeed they
all had a part in the American Catholic success story. And all can
be helpful as we attempt to encourage Catholics to engage issues of
global warming and environmental justice.

Naming an Evil and Demanding Action

I think we can draw from this experience at least one important lesson for our work to renew American Catholic social thought and
action. That lesson was put well by the German theologian Karl
Rahner many years ago. It is possible, in the name of the faith,
Rahner wrote, to *name* an evil. It is also possible, in the name of
the faith, to demand *action,* for Christians must struggle against
evil. But it is not possible, in the name of the faith, to say what
that action must be.[4] For example, racism is evil, one must struggle
for integration and solidarity, but it is not clear that busing or affir-
mative action or hate crime legislation is the best way to overcome
that evil.

Let us look at each part. The church helps us name social injustice, and as a church we have some unique resources: our historical
memory, our presence among so many classes and social groups, our
global reach, our ability to invite dialogue, and our comprehensive
body of social teaching. The church agitates the public conscience
and educates people about injustice, often simply by giving voice to
the voiceless. We have enormous potential here to offer a unique
perspective on environmental justice issues, and to lend legitimacy
to reform efforts. The church also helps us in the demand for action.
For example the Catholic Peacebuilding Network seeks to move
beyond stale arguments about just war and pacifism to recover the
more basic call to peacemaking, an effort embodied in grassroots
work for peace in terribly violent situations across the globe. Similarly the Catholic Coalition on Climate Change spins off a variety of
projects aimed at translating work for just and sustainable environmental reform into concrete action. But no one knows better than
those on the ground the truth of Rahner's third point that particular
projects should not be labeled as the way required by faith. Instead
lay people, in families and neighborhoods, at work and in the vol-
untary organizations of civil society, and in politics, are the subjects

who act. They are agents of transformation, drawing on their experience and expertise, working with others of diverse interests and beliefs, making their best judgment as to what is to be done. Our central question then, what are we to do about global warming, requires for our church a genuine option for the laity as laity, as citizens sharing responsibility for their communities and our world.

Lessons for the Environmental Justice Movement

First, the most important challenge is learning how to live together and share responsibility for a common life when we have very serious differences. That is the challenge of solidarity on the ground. It is a challenge in the contemporary church as well as outside the church. We used to say that the church must be just in its own practices if it was to preach justice in the world. Now we need to add that we must embody solidarity — unity, common good, shared responsibility — in our own life if we are to witness to it, promote it, teach it, in our civic life.

Second, as the Holy Father's teaching on gift, and economy of communion, in his recent encyclical *Caritas in Veritate,* and his less systematic reflections on nonviolence suggest, we need to re-center our imaginations on the promises embodied in our faith. As Sister Joan Chittister suggested recently, if we really think about our commitment to the Gospel vision of the Kingdom of God, we would all know how far we are from it and we might recover a sense of humility in our spirit and our discourse.[5] Maybe Dorothy Day and Peter Maurin, and in another way Thomas Merton, are at the center, and it is the rest of us who are on the edge.

Third, we need to think about how to develop a politics of solidarity and the common good here in the United States in this new globalized world. We don't teach civics well, perhaps, because we ourselves are not really sure what is to be done. Isaiah's peaceable kingdom, a symbol of God's intention for a just, peaceful, and sustainable world seems a long way from even the best cap and trade bills to curb emissions and halt further global warming. And getting that bill is really hard. What to do about that has something to do with recovering a sense of thick citizenship, where personal, business, professional, and civic lives are all shaped by the common good. Remember the Ralph Nader of earlier years, inspiring young lawyers and scientists to give a few years to defending the public interest, organizing citizen action to get us to send a few dollars to pay professionals to defend our common interests in the halls of government and regulatory agencies and before corporations. Think of older ideas of vocation, when social as well as personal ethics informed medical, legal, engineering, and other professions. That is a task of cultural, educational, and religious reconstruction that could serve the public interests.

A Concluding Meditation on History and Responsibility

Nowadays a lot of Catholics believe that they and their church have become too American, and they must recover a sense of distinctive Catholic identity. This widely felt need is often tied to an American Catholic story of uncritical accommodation to American society and culture. If the American Catholic story is one of accommodation to American culture, which is now found wanting, even a "culture of death," then it may well be that the best way to mobilize Catholics for action is to rally them around our Catholic standard to witness to our truth and invite consideration of Catholic teaching as an alternative to prevailing American practice. That approach, it seems to me, is closely associated with the anti-abortion and anti-gay marriage movements, which have come to dominate Catholic discourse. They have done so in part because even those who prefer the Bernardin version of the consistent ethic of life accept the idea that the historical story is one of accommodation and the prescription is a recovery of identity and integrity through the assertion of difference, counter-cultural in purpose and rhetoric, subcultural in practice. Unfortunately Catholic environmental reform efforts, with their emphasis on solidarity, shared responsibility and the common good, will be hampered by that story.

I would tell the story of American Catholicism differently, of Americanization as the achievement of goals actively pursued, and still pursued, by American Catholic families. If liberation consists of poor and marginalized people achieving economic security, upward social mobility, access to dominant institutions, political participation, and cultural respect, then for millions of Catholic families the story is one of liberation. The fruit of liberation is the freedom we see all around us: people choose, even their religious identity. And the flip side of liberation is responsibility. This is our country now; we have helped make it what it is, and we share responsibility for what it will become. The headline of a few years ago — "Bishops Blame Society" — will not do. Shared social and political responsibility is a fact and not an option: the option is whether or not to accept responsibility and act on it with intelligent dedication to the common life and the common good. We got here in part by choosing solidarity with one another as a way to achieve solidarity with our fellow Americans. The environmental reflection we have engaged in calls us to recognize that solidarity and build from it a solidarity with the entire human family. But the story, the frame, of our self-understanding must open us to that solidarity, not turn us in on ourselves. Let us pray that we all can make our own the opening words of the Second Vatican Council's Pastoral Constitution on the Church and the Modern World: "The joys and the hopes, the griefs and anxieties, of the men [and women] of this age, especially those who are poor or in any way afflicted, are the joys and the hopes, the griefs and anxieties of the followers of Christ."[6]

Notes

1. For a history of social action see David O'Brien *Public Catholicism: American Catholics and Public Life, 1789 to 1989* (New York: Macmillan, 1989)

2. See Anthony Burke Smith, *The Look of Catholics: Portrayals in Popular Culture from the Great Depression to the Cold War* (Lawrence: University Press of Kansas, 2010).

3. "Stewards of Creation," *America,* April 20–27, 2009.

4. Karl Rahner, *The Christian Commitment,* trans. Cecily Hastings (New York: Sheed & Ward, 1962), 29.

5. Joan Chittister, O.S.B., "Pride and Humility," *National Catholic Reporter,* July 8, 2009.

6. Walter M. Abbott, ed., *The Documents of Vatican II* (New York: America Press, 1966), 199.

SEVEN

Panel Discussion

Attendees at the conference, September 26, 2009, were asked to write down questions on note cards. These note cards were submitted to the moderator, Richard Miller, who selected the questions based on how often particular questions or related questions were asked by attendees at the conference.

Richard Miller: Dr. Bergant, could you please comment on the Genesis text on human beings having dominion over creation?

Dianne Bergant: We have traditionally read this text literally. If we are going to read it from a historical point of view, there is enough evidence within the whole creation narrative (Gen. 1:1–2:48) to suggest that behind that story is the theme of monarchy. In the Ancient Near Eastern world, monarchs were the ones who subdued and had dominion. There are all kinds of pictures about that. Also in the Ancient Near Eastern world, people had the custom of setting up an image of their god, or an image of their king. Not idols. They may have deteriorated to idolatry, but these were images that functioned to indicate where the king ruled supreme or where the god ruled supreme, something very similar to a national flag, which is a symbol of sovereignty. Also in the Ancient Near Eastern world, people did believe that their kings were, in a very real sense, images of god, if not gods themselves, so there is enough historical background to suggest that what we have there (though you don't always have obvious language or language that is obvious to us), you have a royal theme. Now in ancient Israel, kings are not divine, and in ancient Israel, kings are also under the responsibility of obeying the law. So what Israel has is not only royalty that has responsibility for the natural world, but royalty that is accountable to God for the way they exercise that responsibility. Which means that "subdue and have dominion" within this theological context means "do it the way God would do it in God's stead." Today we would refer to that as witness, that we are witnesses. If we proclaim our God is compassionate, then the only way that our claim can be valid is if we are compassionate because the compassion of God is witnessed by the way we live our lives and the goodness of God is witnessed, not on a paper, but by the lives of individuals. So in that sense then "subdue and have dominion" means "act in the world the way God would" and then of course one would say that God created the world so that it would thrive, increase, multiply, and fill the earth. God did not create the world so that God could exploit it. Therefore, draw the conclusion that that really calls us to act in the world in God's stead and allow the world to thrive. That is chapter 1!

Richard Miller: Dr. O'Keefe, which of the models you spoke of best captures or articulates the social/personal dimension of resurrection?

John O'Keefe: I actually think the third one is the best model because I'm so attracted to Irenaean eschatology. I do not know why, but I have always been sort of interested in the resurrection of the body. I remember when I was in graduate school, I took a class on eschatology, and we were reading 1 Corinthians 15, and I thought, "He is talking about bodies." I had thought throughout my life that resurrection was simply some kind of spiritual event. After that class I went back to our apartment, I was newly married at the time, and I said to my wife, "You know, I think this is about bodies." She responded, "Well, who cares? You know it doesn't really matter, you are just going to get to heaven, it doesn't really matter." I have thought about this a lot over the years and it does matter. It really has to do with love and concern for individuals. I think one of the great insights of the Christian religion is the commitment to particular things and particular people, and a reverence for them, and this kind of desire for them to be preserved in some way. I do not mean this in some sort of literal way necessarily; I do not know what it actually means to talk about a resurrected person, but this idea that their identity — the people we love, our children, our parents, our grandparents — at the end of the day is somehow preserved in God and in God's future is important. For me, in some ways the whole social project of Christianity is based on that. In the ancient empire, you didn't have social services. The Christians, taking it from the Jews, really took concern for people, for individuals, and ran with it, because they really believed in the value of individual human beings. I think this runs through the whole tradition. That is why I am really resistant to any idea that there is some kind of absorption of identity in heaven. I think this is a particularly important insight of the Christian faith.

Richard Miller: Dr. Schaefer, sinning requires freedom, but where is the person's freedom in social sin?

Jame Schaefer: When we think of freedom and making decisions, we assume that we have the capability to make informed decisions. Freedom is still operative in social sin, because underlying social sin, as the magisterial teaching of the church stresses, is individual responsibility. Individual responsibility is not absent in social sin and it would behoove us when we are facing huge questions like climate change that are so complex, with information from so many different disciplines, to at least strive to first of all know what we are doing individually that might be sinful from a planetary perspective and then to identify what we could do to change. But it would also mean to look at how other people are caught in these structures of sin that will perpetuate this ongoing planetary sinning. So there is always individual responsibility. We are always individually responsible for whatever we are doing that is contributing to climate change and is affecting people today, especially the poor and vulnerable, people in the future, and the whole planet. So individual responsibility to make informed decisions about what we are doing remains with us but also the responsibility I think to join with others. This is where the principle of solidarity comes in. Join with others in recognizing our cumulative sinfulness that brings about these structures of sin in which people get enmeshed and then keep on perpetuating planetary sinfulness. So we are really following the principle of subsidiarity now, working at all levels. At bottom, however, it is up to each one of us individually to examine our conscience, to examine our way of life, to examine our attitudes, and then to respond accordingly. But we have to realize that we can't just do it alone. We need to work together; we need to move to another level of collectivity, whether it is in our family, our place of work, our community. We need to examine our consciences as to how we are contributing to these planetary problems and how, then, we can work in the various aspects of community to address them.

Richard Miller: This question is for Dr. Schaefer and Dr. Finn. Is our present economic framework structurally sinful?

Daniel Finn: Yes and no. I mean we have to talk about particulars, right? What parts of it are we talking about? I would look at those structures of expectations, both cultural and economic, market-based and habit-based in a culture, that lead us to do destructive things to other people, to the environment, but that isn't everything. Markets, of course, are very large and complicated. They have some incentives that are really fine; other incentives that are quite negative. The struggle for structuring our economy properly involves a series of debates over what to allow within that market that is defining the legal parameters within which the market functions. We each have to live out our own moral lives because, of course, moral standards are much higher than legal standards. The most basic issues of morality get worked out in terms of the law. What abuses are so severe that we are going to make them illegal in some way, and, of course we have not done that really well in lots of ways. So yes, some of those parts of our economic structure would be characterized as sinful, but by no means all of them, in this sense. It is an analogical use of the term, but I think quite an accurate one.

Jame Schaefer: Dan, of course, is the economics expert, but one of the things that I've been concerned with is that often in making decisions in the economy about what companies and public utilities and so forth are going to do, what kind of energy sources they are going to be relying upon to generate electricity, they do not take marginal environmental costs into consideration. And these marginal costs, like social costs, are left on the outskirts, and it takes public service commissions of the various states to identify what those costs might be. In the case of human-forced climate change these costs are considerable when they are spread out over long periods of time. The different models used for identifying these costs come up with ranges, of course, rather than some conclusive figure or some conclusive action. So I think we can build into our economic structures social costs and these marginal environmental costs if we mandate that they are to be included. How do we get things mandated to be included? Through people acting with their representatives and their various legislative bodies to make sure that they are included. We need to demand that our represen- tatives at various levels of government — from municipal, county, state, regional, and of course federal — factor social and marginal costs, into things like the construction of a nuclear power plant or the construction of another dirty coal plant or any major project that is going to affect the environment and all constituents of the environment. If those social and marginal environmental costs are not factored in to a particular project they are going to be hidden costs, and they will be costs that people in the future are going to have to pay. We have to pay it now in the form of all the carbonic compounds we are putting into the air with coal. We have to pay it now with all the high-level nuclear wastes that are accumulating at nuclear power plants and going nowhere. They are staying right at the plants, out in the open, on concrete slabs in these silos. These are just a couple of examples of costs that had not been identified and now are going to be highly costly in the future. So we need to demand that these social costs and marginal costs are factored in to avoid the structures of sin that are only going to perpetuate these problems.

John O'Keefe: At the risk of self-promotion, I have a podcast, which is basically an Internet talk show, with a colleague. We recently interviewed another of my colleagues on the pope's new encyclical. It really has a lot to say about markets, and I think it is really worth reading. But one of the things my colleagues I interviewed pointed out is that the pope sort of says a lot of us in the modern world think of markets as if they were some kind of pagan gods that we need to venerate or they will get mad at us and get back at us. The pope reminds us that the markets are actually human creations, and therefore human beings can actually intervene in them. I found that to be really helpful. [The website is *http://cct.creighton.edu/*]

Richard Miller: Dr. O'Brien, as lay people, how do we build the institutions within the church and society to allow for mobilization?

David O'Brien: There was a day when I was more optimistic answering questions like this than I am now. I really am not terribly sure how to advise people these days to act within the church. I do think that it is remarkable that over the last ten years a whole series of things have happened in the Catholic Church that people have really done nothing about. You could walk into a middle-class parish and people would complain and say this is not a good thing; you could go to a Catholic college or university and you would meet people and they would say it is not a good thing, but people basically did nothing. Now let us take two examples. First, after the sex abuse crisis broke into the public in 2002, people in Boston organized a group called Voice of the Faithful, and they tried to go national with it. I should note, for full disclosure purposes, that at one point I served on their board of trustees. It was stunning to me how few people I knew joined it — people of distinction, academics, theologians, Catholic teachers, people who work for the church, Catholic professionals, Catholic lay people. They said it was a good thing. They said that it was a good thing lay people are doing something. They complained about some of the steps that it took, not appreciating the fact that these were all amateurs who did not know their way around church politics, and they were saddened when the outcome of the sex abuse crisis was less positive than it should have been.

If you think the sex abuse crisis was handled well and resolved properly by the bishops, you simply are not paying attention. The way it was handled was a disaster. And we still have not fully paid the price of it all. The National Review Board brought out the John Jay Report in February 2004, and also brought out an interim report on "Causes and Consequences" from a subcommittee chaired by attorney Robert Bennett. That Bennett report laid out a number of questions that needed to be confronted that were never confronted. That report just sank like a stone, and intelligent, engaged, serious Catholics said nothing. And let it all go. They let the whole thing go.

When you think about it, what are the major changes that have taken place? There have been seminary changes, they are more conservative. We have had a year of the Eucharist and a year of the Priest. There have been changes in the practice of the Eucharist in our churches, which have downgraded and held at bay lay Eucharistic ministers. In my diocese, they can't even use the key in the tabernacle anymore. So nobody did anything about it. In 2004, the Catholic bishops' document *Faithful Citizenship* was hijacked by a very well organized, admirably organized, conservative group. Cardinal McCarrick was attacked in full-page ads in the press, and very little was done by Catholics in this country to defend him. I could give other examples and they are all very, very discouraging. The ongoing inquiry into the Sisters is another example, which I have written about on the *NCR* website. How many people have spoken up in defense of the Sisters? How many people have pointed out that this is not one step, but it has been a whole history of Vatican interference with the Sisters, and no one does anything? So I'm a little pessimistic in answering this question. Why aren't the young people doing something? People do not do anything. So I think I have to assume there are not a lot of people out there who take responsibility for the politics of the church. They are quite resigned to treat the church like a monarchy. There is the famous cover of *Commonweal* magazine, my favorite Catholic magazine, with the headline "Are the Bishops Listening?" That is the politics of a royal court.

So what should Catholics do? I would say look for independent ways to organize yourselves as Catholics to take on serious questions in church and society. Look at the movements like Focolare, Sant'Egidio, and some of the other remarkable movements in the church in other parts of the world. These provide a way of engaging and practicing your faith that maybe go around a little bit the way some of the church structures work. It would be good to find people to renew Catholic publications to create a public life in the church so that the church's officials are held accountable for their actions. Catholics in Alliance for the Common Good was an effort to provide public support for the basic Bernardin era understanding of the seamless garment of life in an independent political presentation of church teaching. Again, very few people sent a check or joined. So there are opportunities out there with Voice of the Faithful, The Catholics in Alliance for the Common Good, and with international groups like Focolare and Sant'Egidio, which are growing a little bit in this country. The question is to take personal responsibility and find ways that grassroots movements and national leadership can challenge what is going on.

Richard Miller: This question is for everyone on the panel. Is there a list of resources, websites, organizations, periodicals, books that any of you could share with today's group?

John O'Keefe: The website from which David's handout comes, the Catholic Coalition on Climate Change, is really fantastic and has lots of resources; a lot of church documents are gathered there. I think that is a really good place to start if you are interested in what the church has to say about this. And then there are just tons of things out there that are not necessarily religiously oriented but are very helpful in learning more about what is going on in the world environmentally. The Catholic Coalition on Climate Change is a really good website [*www.catholicsandclimatechange.org/*]. I actually interviewed the director of it on the podcast so you can find out about what he is doing. He is a really good guy.

Dianne Bergant: In addition to that, I think sometimes all you have to do is just do an Internet search by typing in "Catholic and ecology" and it is amazing! You get a lot of junk as well. That is always the problem. If you are not acquainted with what is going on, you really don't always know what is good and what is really over the edge, the wrong edge.

Jame Schaefer: I have had a succession of honors programs students and graduate students work on the various documents issued by popes and by bishops around the world. If you are interested in seeing what they have to say about the environment you can go to that website: *www.inee.mu.edu,* which is about three years old. There are more documents that I would like to have put online or at least have my students find to put online that popes and bishops have issued. One thing I'm waiting for, and I'm very excited to see happen. I heard from Charles Murphy up in Maine that the pope is going to give the World Day of Peace address on the environment. That is twenty years after Pope John Paul II put out his statement on the environment for the 1990 World Day of Peace, which was called "Peace with God the Creator, Peace with All Creation."

Dianne Bergant: You know it is not uncommon that the January World Day of Peace proclamation of the pope has something to say on ecology. Not the whole thing, but if you look at past statements, you will find some things about ecology.

Jame Schaefer: John Paul II's statement was the first statement by a pope dedicated on the environment, so if Benedict follows up, that will be just great, a twenty-year celebration.

David O'Brien: There is a lot going on with food questions around the country too. In local communities, everywhere we go we meet young people, often very highly educated people, who are going back to the land and trying to do local agricultural projects. National Catholic Rural Life Conference is a great network of news and information about food issues around the country. I will tell a little story. I had breakfast the other day with a young woman who graduated from Holy Cross about seven or eight years ago, one of our great graduates. Then later on she was in the master's program, the remarkable master's program in international peace studies at the Kroc Institute at Notre Dame. I said, "What are you going to do now?" She said she was going to Iowa, to Dubuque, to a farm, where a bunch of Catholic Worker intellectual types are getting together now, where there has been quite a successful Catholic Worker farm. They are going to finally create Peter Maurin's agronomic university. I thought that was kind of neat.

Dianne Bergant: A little bit of bragging too. There are several religious communities that have such farms as part of their ministry as well. I would suggest (though I don't know your diocese well) that you find out what offices are available in this diocese and neighboring dioceses, particularly relative to the issue of food in farming dioceses and find out what is available there and what they are doing in those kinds of programs. And it will be amazing what you find is being done!

Jame Schaefer: And ask that your diocesan newspaper put a little section there that will link you to those kinds of sites because that can be very helpful.

Richard Miller: I would just add that you can write down your name and email in one of the binders in the back and I will email you a list of organizations. Let me just name a few here though. The Sierra Club has a whole campaign (*www.sierraclub.org/Coal/*), which has been quite successful, against coal-fire-powered plants because coal is perhaps the most important part of the problem. It is very important to make sure we do not have any more coal plants built and there has been a lot of success keeping about a 100 of the 150 coal plants that were in the planning phase from being built. There is 350.org (*www.350.org*) and wecansolveit.org (*www.wecansolveit.org*). For further questions concerning the range of issues surrounding sustainability it is hard to beat the Earth Policy Institute (*www.earth-policy.org/*), which also has a PowerPoint presentation available to spread the word as does 350.org. Another thing of interest relates to Dr. O'Brien's talk about solidarity with people you disagree with on some issues. I would say that many of the environmental groups have a wonderful sense of the common good, and Catholics could easily enter into that world and partner with these organizations that are well established so we do not have to reinvent the wheel.

Richard Miller: What ways would you suggest that participants at this conference could work together to address the issues raised today?

John O'Keefe: I think that the first thing is to try to change yourself. This turns out to be incredibly hard. I first started by carrying canvas bags to the grocery store, and then, you know, I would always forget them in the car, and then I got to the point where I forced myself to go back to the car and get them and leave the groceries there, so now I never forget. Then we, my family, decided we would cut our energy consumption as much as possible. We had a hot tub, and when I found out how much power it used, we unplugged it. That didn't go over so well with the kids, but we did it anyway. And so you take these steps. And then I started buying meat from a farmer I know in Iowa. There are these kinds of personal things you can do and you can tap into the church's tradition of asceticism. But certainly pay attention to what the major issues are. And right now — I mean right now! — is the time for this climate legislation. If we miss the opportunity in the next month, it could be ten years before the United States Congress gets to it. This is politically urgent, so I think we have got to pay attention to what is going on in government and act.

Dianne Bergant: Walk! How many times do we take a car for a couple of blocks, and we could have walked. And I'm not even talking about "therefore, don't use gasoline!" If we don't walk, we don't live as long as we might be able to if we did walk. Are we not funny people? We eat and eat and eat and then complain that we gain weight, and then we buy machines that help us to walk stairs instead of walking the stairs. I say it facetiously and I realize, people will say, "But I have arthritis." You know what I'm talking about. This is something that is so much a part of our lifestyle that we do not realize what a significant change it is to walk. People will also say, the best exercise is not running; it is walking and you live longer and it takes off the fat and it strengthens your heart, to say nothing about lessening our carbon footprint. So I would suggest a four-letter word: Walk!

David O'Brien: That is good. You know, if I were forty years younger, I would say, I don't know what the situation is here in

Kansas City but in a local community, a group could get together under the banner of the Catholic Coalition of Climate Change and the St. Francis Pledge (see *www.catholicsandclimatechange.org/*), and just make an announcement that you exist, and in a community this size, you would certainly find, I think, a lot of people — schoolteachers, people in various business situations, that are very interested in this stuff and would be interested in kind of a Catholic gathering of people, maybe support for projects they are already doing and some networking that could take place. I think in most communities now there are an awful lot of people doing some remarkable things in energy conservation and all the rest, and putting up a banner and inviting people would probably be a nice first step.

Daniel Finn: While we are talking about short words, I'll talk about a three-letter word, and that is "tax." For some reason, taxes have gotten a very bad image in popular culture. It is not often that we stand up and say: "Wait a minute! You know taxes are an appropriate part of life, and if we need to do something and don't have enough money in the city council or in the state legislature we need to raise our taxes to get it done." This is part of the common good. If you think those common conditions of social life have to be there for us to live a full life, we have to be willing to pay for it. Dealing with environmental problems is going to cost something in terms of our economic productivity, not very much, frankly. I think estimates are that it is going to cost us a few percentage points of our gross domestic product, a couple of percent for all the things we have done so far and it may be that it is going to cost us more than that, of course, in the future. But it is sort of a cost of doing business if we want to keep our world going to be able to provide the money to our public authorities to subsidize the appropriate technologies, to pay for all the kinds of experimentation that needs to happen, and that is going to cost money and we can't do it with a bake sale. It is going to have to be taxation, and somehow we need to change the culture on how people think about taxes. They are not terrible things.

David O'Brien: You could add the word "eat." The Catholic Rural Life Conference has a great project called "Eating as a Moral Act," and they will give you great literature. If you want to educate people quickly, just go through a process like that.

Richard Miller: I would add to what John was saying. I received a phone call right before I came here from *wecansolveit.org*. They said that the bill for cap and trade is actually headed to the Senate on Monday; I haven't been able to check that, I just got the message. So this is underway. Again, phone calls are worth a lot; they are a big deal. All you have to do is an Internet search and type in "US Senate" and you will find the phone number of your senators. I actually have the phone numbers of your senators. If you want their number I can give it to you after this discussion.

Richard Miller: Dr. Finn, how are corporations going to count the economic value and cost of natural resources?

Daniel Finn: There's a story. There was an effort once by a number of economists that tried to estimate the combined value of the natural world to human life: What is it worth? The number they came up with was something like $450 trillion, to which another economist said, "That is a pretty good approximation of infinity, right?" You know, life is unthinkable without the natural world, and yet we have this instinct to try to monetize it simply because when you are dealing with public policy, you are dealing with consequentialist thinking. It isn't just a matter of intentions. You have to ask: What will be the consequence of this and that? And so we are forced into this sort of reductionism of very important values, to talk about them in some sort of numerical fashion to compare quite different things. And so, at times, that has to be actually worked out in detail. Other times it can be done without computing the particular numbers, but to say that certain procedures can't be used any more, certain ways of doing things need to be done. Cap in trade is a good suggestion, a good example of a process that will, in fact, be monetized. These permits for pollution will have values and that value will slowly rise over time to get firms to pollute less and less as time goes on. And so at times it is important to get some financial estimate of the damage being done, and I think that lies behind the cap and trade process. At other times, it is not so necessary, so I think it depends on the context. I think we have to take it one issue at a time.

Richard Miller: Can we purify and recover the notion of stewards of creation in such a way as to take into account both technologies and the inherent value of every element of the web of life?

John O'Keefe: One thing I've noticed is that in the sort of nonreligious environmental community, or in sort of the old environmental community maybe, there is a little bit of utopianism. A couple of years ago I went to DC to visit my daughter when she was in college. We went to this Green America Event, which used to be Co-op America. It is a big conference. And there were all these people dressed in Eastern-like monastic costumes selling ointments and things like that. This kind of represented the old green movement, and then at another part of the conference they were having workshops on insulating your house. I think this represents the change that is going on in the environmental world. Stewardship is the model emerging as a responsible way of human beings living on Earth. We are not going to build utopian communities where we suddenly dismantle modern society and get rid of technology and go back to living on collective farms. It is just not going to happen. I think my own reading of the new papal encyclical really underscores that the model is appropriate human interaction with the environment and appropriate human cultivation of the earth. The pope has a whole chapter on the environment, which I think is the longest sustained discussion of the environment in any magisterial document. It definitely is the stewardship model, and I think that is helpful and appropriate.

Dianne Bergant: I agree with you. There is, however, another image that I think, at least for me, is very useful. Paul uses the image of the human body in order to talk about the community. The image says, and I am paraphrasing: Can the hand say to the foot, "I have no need of you because you are not a hand?" Every part of the body really works for the good of the body. Now, no one will deny that you can live without a hand but you cannot live without a head. And it is not a question of hierarchy; it is a question of being responsible for certain functions that are essential for the fundamental life of the whole body. Now, I'm suggesting, take that image of body and expand it and think of that image of body as not just the body of the church or the body of the human race, but the body of the natural world, which means that one, in a certain sense, playfully can say, "Can the human being say to the bumblebee, 'I have no need of you because you are not a human; therefore, you are not valuable.'" Of course, now we know, no bumblebees, no pollination; no pollination, no food; no food, no human beings. So there is a kind of synergistic relationship, interrelationship. I realize this is simplistic, but all images are. I think if we could maybe begin to think of that metaphor — body — we might begin then to realize a scratch on our finger can kill us. And it may very well be that the demise of part of the land or the demise of certain animals can kill us. It would help us if we would begin to see this kind of interdependency. I don't think we as a race are really used to thinking about being interdependent. We are not even used to thinking about interdependency with each other, to say nothing about expanding that image. So I find returning to this image every once in awhile is very helpful. Again it is a question of expanding our imagination; we are not imaginative people. Where did we lose that along the way? We were born with it. Look at the children! But if we would expand our imagination and really begin to think with different images it would help us. I personally find that image of the body very helpful. It doesn't say everything, but no image does. But it really does help sometimes to recognize that we are dependent. It is not just that they are dependent on us (the other members of the natural world), in fact, some deep ecologists (and I don't hold this) say the worst thing that has happened to the natural world is the appearance of human beings.

Jame Schaefer: Then do you think that the human being is the head of the body?

Dianne Bergant: Well, we do that with the church, you know. And that would say that some members of the body have certain functions or responsibilities that affect the fundamental functioning of the whole. So I'm not sure. Are trees going to undermine the sustainability of the world the same way as human beings? I don't think so. And again, I realize an image has its limitations, but I just find that, if we think again about stewardship, it implies responsibility and accountability, and that is us. We are responsible but also accountable.

Jame Schaefer: I do a lot of modeling with my students and also in my research looking at certain patristic and medieval notions and also looking at the various statements by bishops and popes. One of the statements we look at is that of the U.S. Catholic bishops on renewing the earth, in which the human being is modeled as a cocreator and steward. Every time I teach my course on foundations for ecological ethics, my students dislike both of those models. This is because steward puts us apart from and managing over the natural world, even if we add "managing over with responsibility and accountability." It still does not put us within the natural world and does not sufficiently recognize our interconnectedness and interdependence. One of the models that my students have particularly liked is that of the virtuous cooperator, that is, the human being who sees himself and herself as an intelligent cooperator who is making informed decisions on how to cooperate with other species and ecological systems and the biosphere. Behavior then is oriented toward the moral virtues, in particular grounded especially in the theological virtue of love. That particular model seems to encapsulate a number of things: it comes from the tradition, it is informed by and parallel with our scientific findings (at least basic scientific findings), it is relevant to the ecological crisis that we are facing, and it is helpful. It is helpful because it points to a way that helps us act prudently (and that is a huge virtue: moderately, justly, with courage, and I would add humbly, one of the seven cardinal virtues). Modeling is very important, and I think we have to rethink ourselves. As a matter of fact, I really believe as a theologian that the basis of our environmental problems is in how we think about ourselves. We need to think about ourselves as interconnected with, a part of, contributing in some way or another, contributing by knowing what technology is going to be appropriate to use. We need to follow this wonderful line of prudent decision-making that we find especially in Thomas Aquinas, motivated by the virtue of love, love of neighbor, love of God. I have lots of reservations about this notion of steward, and I don't know if it can be purified. It would take a lot of effort to purify it, but I don't think it takes us deeply enough into our sense of radical dependence upon other species, the air, the land, the water; interconnectedness, interrelatedness with other beings. That is my take on modeling. I think we have a long way to go but thinking how we think about ourselves is really crucial in this day of environmental degradation.

Daniel Finn: But Jame, let me just ask a question. It seems to me that "cooperator" cannot name well our relationship with the rest of nature in that we have a capacity of transcendence, to stand back and ask: Of all the mistakes we have made, which one should we stop making? That is not true for the eagle that preys on the bird. It is not true for the fox that takes the squirrel. If they overeat and there is a local environmental collapse of a certain ecosystem, we do not blame them for eating too much. This is just nature, and we have a different kind of capacity and a different kind of responsibility than any of those other creatures will ever have. I think "stewardship" tries to get that and "cooperator" pretends it is not there, as if we're equal cooperators. And we can't be equal cooperators, can we?

Jame Schaefer: No, we are cooperators according to our distinctiveness as creatures, and that is what I'm saying. This is where we would be, allegedly, the informed cooperator who goes through this process of prudent decision-making to assure justice, especially for the poor, to function in a sustainable way ourselves, taking from other species and the air, the land, and the water, like animals take to sustain themselves. Seldom do you find animals that are excessive because they eat what they need to sustain themselves. There you have this dynamic development of ecological systems accordingly. So it is cooperation on the basis of the innate capabilities of the creature. We should be the informed virtuous cooperators.

Dianne Bergant: That is why I like the idea of body, because the same stuff flows through us as flows through them as it does with a body. I think this discussion is very helpful to show the limitations of certain models, but they are all limited. Every model is limited. They can all look at a certain thing at a certain dimension but then they leave others out. It is not so much a question (and I don't think you would say this) of either/or; it is a question of both/and. And there are other images or models that could be helpful. I think we are all saying we have to think about ourselves differently, not as the pinnacle of creation, at the top of the pyramid and looking down on everything else. That is how I learned science. At the bottom of creation is inanimate creation and above it is vegetative and above that is, you know, all the way up and then at the top you have human beings and then there is even a hierarchy there, and then up at the top you have angels. We learned that, and that is almost instilled in us as a model, but that is not a helpful model. It does say some things, but it doesn't say everything. It may say that the higher up you get (even that language!) it becomes more complex, but it does not mean it is better. But we think, of course, it is better because we are at the top! So those models say something but not everything. And we have institutionalized some models that have not been very helpful for us as part of and a very significant part of the natural world.

John O'Keefe: Just one more thought on that. I too have had periods of resisting stewardship because you think about, say, the Andromeda galaxy, and we are not stewards of the Andromeda galaxy. And we are not really stewards of even our own solar system. When the sun becomes a red giant, we will not be able do anything about it. I heard an argument that really helped me to just accept stewardship as a kind of act of practical wisdom. This is the language of many, many Christians in the world, and it is certainly a concept that people can get their minds around and understand. That makes sense to me, and it certainly is, I think, the language that at least the current leadership of the church is opting to use.

Richard Miller: Dr. O'Keefe, how do you reconcile Irenaeus of Lyon's worldview with the modern scientific one? And do you see equality, in the terminology that Dr. Schaefer introduced, between the old poor (i.e., people) and the new poor (i.e., endangered species)?

John O'Keefe: As for the first part, I don't know how to reconcile it with modern science. Part of the eco-mysticism that I like is this sense of the participation of all creatures in this sort of mystical reality of God's creation. The classical Christian narrative is that God is going to change that in some way, that we're going to overcome death at the end and God is going to reconstitute everything and this gives you these very literal visions of resurrection. So I guess I'm still thinking about that and what the implications are. But for me, deep in the Christian imagination is this idea that something's broken. Theologians debate about whether or not human sin broke creation or whether human sin just broke our relationship with creation, but certainly the theology of Irenaeus, and you see this in the late Augustine, really saw salvation as fixing our relationship with creation and that Christ is the key to repairing that relationship. I think part of the impulse behind social justice is that things are broken and need to be repaired. It is not like we're just going to sit around and say, "Well, we need to adjust our attitude to the world," which I think is characteristic of many Eastern traditions. Christianity deep down has this idea we have got to fix it because God is going to fix it and we need to model that. I don't know exactly how to reconcile these two yet; I'm thinking about it.

The second thing, no, I don't think that the ethics are exactly the same. The scenario you sometimes hear from deep ecologists is that if you are on a boat at sea with a puppy and a baby and you have to sacrifice one, that the moral choice would be hard. And I say the moral choice would not be hard. You save the baby, not the puppy. But that doesn't mean that the puppy has no rights at all and that the puppy doesn't make a claim on us. I think that the person to read on this is Aldo Leopold. We need to start thinking about the natural world as a subject that makes a moral claim but not necessarily the same moral claim that our children make on us.

Dianne Bergant: I think when we talk about the world broken by sin and then put back together by Christianity, and I say this as a faithful Christian, we must remember that all of those stories come from ancient Mesopotamian myths. We talk about conquering death; that comes from an ancient myth where the gods were fighting and the god that was killed was Mote, which is Death. So, again, I think that much of what have become problems in contemporary theology, you can trace back to the origin, and we find that our religious ancestors reinterpreted somebody else's theology, which we have done as well. For example, the whole idea of the fall. I keep telling my students, there is no fall! What did they fall from? Look at the story. There was no fall. Sin, yes, but fall presumes fall from grace. That is not ancient Israelite theology; it is Christian theology. And I have no problem with Christian theology so long as we realize when it comes into the picture. That is what I meant when I said we read everything into the story. There is no fall in the Genesis creation narrative. There is a sin. There is no apple, and there is no pomegranate. People are so concerned that it wasn't an apple tree because the ancient Israelites did not have apple trees. They had pomegranate trees. It was the tree of knowledge of good and evil. What kind of fruit is that? It is a mythical story that talks about honest-to-God struggle, but we have once again institutionalized and concretized some beautiful imagery. I know that is now part of our tradition and that is fine. I am not challenging the tradition because I do believe that we have sinned. I do not know if we have fallen. I do not know if creation in the beginning was ever perfect. It was good, the text says, but perfect and then broken? I don't know. I'm saying, particularly now with the little bit I know about new science and an evolving universe, I don't know if it was perfect in the beginning. And that is an example of how, with new insights into new sciences, we are going to have to really look at our theology and ask how we reinterpret the theology we have been raised on. To which I would give my life. But how do we interpret it in a way that is faithful to the fundamental theological meaning, not necessarily the literary meaning, but the fundamental theological meaning and the reality of the world in which we find it? It is a challenge. And again, this is something that I as a theologian struggle with. So much of the theology that I have learned is really a reinterpretation of earlier theology, which is good. But what we have done (and I'm not sure who the "we" is; we have generations that we can blame besides ourselves) is taken some of the details and have made the details of the story the basis of the way we understand our theology. I don't think that is correct.

Richard Miller: Dr. Finn, why does the church just develop economic principles instead of a worked-out economic theory that is more tuned to the common good?

Daniel Finn: Well, I'm going to presume by "economic theory" somebody has in mind that which economists do, the discipline of economics itself. And, you know, the church doesn't work out physics or chemistry or sociology or economics. These disciplines have a kind of independence that the church has said it will respect. Now it turns out, of course, that the most popular, so-called mainstream economics has many flaws that many Catholic economists and other Christian economists are quite aware of and many secular economists too. I don't mean to be baptizing the mainstream theory, by any means, but there is a kind of humility that the church has shown, rightfully so, I think, to the insights of the sciences. And while we need to be critical, especially in the social sciences, about the questions of method and so forth, it is not fundamentally a theological undertaking but a scientific one. Therefore, the church should not be proposing, as a church, how economists should do economics. It is, again, sort of like the question of politics. There should be good lay Catholics out there doing it and trying to help clean it up and get it right. But the church itself is not in the business of telling us basic economic theory, it seems to me. General principles about what our moral convictions mean for economic life, absolutely, and that is what Catholic social thought is.

Richard Miller: This is for Dr. Bergant. If in Exodus nature is serving God while in Wisdom nature is following its own laws, where is God in Wisdom? Who is in charge of nature in Wisdom?

Dianne Bergant: I'm not sure what the questioner meant by nature in Wisdom following its own laws. In the Wisdom tradition (this is what makes wisdom creation theology), one could ask a rather simplistic question: Why is the world the way it is? And the answer would be, "Because that is the way God made it." It is as simple as that. In the Wisdom tradition, and in the creation theology that we find in the Wisdom tradition, there is a presumption that this is the way God made things. Very simplistically, when you drop something, why does it go down instead of up? Well, we know why it goes down, with science, and we would also say because that is the way God made it. We may say it is gravity, but I don't think anybody really understands what gravity is. We know how it works but we don't know why it works that way. So in a certain sense, the Wisdom tradition would say the world is the way it is because that is the way God made it. And the first part, read it again please.

Richard Miller: The question contrasts Exodus where, according to the questioner, nature is serving God and the Wisdom tradition where nature is following its own law.

Dianne Bergant: I would say it is an invalid contrast because clearly Wisdom theology would say this is the way God made it, so in a very real sense, Wisdom might be even more "this is the way God made it" than Exodus would be because in the Exodus story it says that there is oppression, which means that this is not the way things should be. So one thing about ancient Israel, the ancient traditional peoples never questioned the existence of God. Never! The question was, "Which god?" The question was never, "Is there a God?" They just took the presence of God and the activity of God and the power of God and all of the attributes that we have learned, whether they used the language or not, they just took it all for granted. The question was always, "Now, which god? Who is your god?" I think all ancient literature has a dimension of religious literature to it because they just presume that there are gods. This could explain also why it is very easy for people who do not believe in God to simply dismiss religious literature. I don't know if that answered the person's question.

Richard Miller: This is for Dr. Finn. What is your economic/ religious view of our macro-economy being dominated by the defense department share of more than 50 percent of the national budget each year? How does it fit into Pope Benedict's view? How does this affect the common good?

Daniel Finn: Leaving aside the percentages, clearly we spend an awful lot of money on the military, and I think this is far beyond an economic issue. It is clearly a cultural one and a political issue, and I'm not sure it is going to change much in the near future. We have tended to be pretty presumptuous about our view of the world and willing to impose it in many parts of the world through military force. You know, even today, the Taliban sound like pretty bad people, but I'm not sure that we are going to have any better luck at this than the Russians had, than Alexander the Great had. This is a very old society that we are working with. So I think that the church's general story about war and about military force is really important here, but we clearly have to find other ways of dealing with the world's problems than turning to the military.

At the same time, I'm not a pacifist, and therefore there are times when I think force is appropriate. Economically speaking, it does eat up a lot of federal money that could be put in other places that could be quite productive. So it clearly has an important impact on what the government is able to do. And of course, our supplying arms to the rest of the world means that there are an awful lot of countries out there that are also spending way too much money on their military budgets, even though their budgets are a lot less than ours. You know, poor countries buying the advanced fighter jets and the rest, it is a terrible, terrible waste. Of course, recent initiatives to find a nuclear-free world are a wonderful step forward. One might hope that at some point we could move to a world where the military becomes a much, much smaller part of what we are up to.

David O'Brien: All economies are political economies. I kept thinking about that when I heard Dr. Finn talking about markets. The question of the defense budget has to be located again within a political framework. The huge question is the character of America's relationship with the rest of the world. At one point in the talk I was preparing for today, I was going to have a little ten-point checklist, and one of the first points on that checklist would be international cooperation, international responsibility. There is no way to deal with global warming or any of these things without international cooperation. Yet our foreign policy, in a number of ways, is directly contrary to that. In addition to the defense budget and the wars that we have carried out in Iraq and Afghanistan, we have hundreds of bases around the world. We have just established a new set of bases in Africa. We are still approaching the whole question of security and the whole question of the nation's place in the world in a very, very militaristic way, which seems to me to be counterproductive to the kind of political cooperation and institution-building necessary to deal with environmental questions and also with large economic justice questions, and even economic self-interest questions in the long run. But we really close our eyes to the enormity of our political/military investment all over the world. It is just remarkable. The president's speech to the United Nations — he has these wonderful speeches — was an appeal to rethink the way in which we approach international responsibility, and God help us to find ways to respond to that.

Richard Miller: I also got a question that I think I have to respond to so someone doesn't leave here depressed. The question is: "It almost sounds too late to stop the ill fate of greenhouse gases because of denial and the time element. Do you see some concrete steps that could reverse this?" It is late, but not too late. Rajendra Pachauri, the head of the IPCC, maintains that the plants we build in the next few years will determine our fate in 2050. Jim Hansen writes a letter to President Obama saying that this is our last chance, Obama's first term is our last chance. Of course, this letter does not appear in our papers, it was in *The Guardian* in England. If you want to know what our scientists are saying you should read *The Guardian*, not our papers. Anyway, they are saying that this is our last chance, these next few years, so it is pretty serious.

Now, I think that you can reverse this. I gave the example of people responding to the bonuses at AIG by flooding Congress with phone calls so that within one day you had Congress on its heels. I think Congress will respond if you push on them. So my recommendation is to tell everybody that you know that this is enormously serious and encourage them to call Congress. Call, call, call! It is very simple. It takes only a few minutes, but is very effective. Also, write letters to your congressional leaders. Letters are very effective. Letters are actually the best way to communicate with Congress. And good old fashioned letters are better than emails. I mentioned a poll of congressional staff from a few years ago that showed this. So yes, the scientists are saying we are very close, but it is not over. So we need to organize, organize, organize, mobilize, mobilize, mobilize.

Well, we have run out of time. Thank you all so much for attending the conference. I want to thank the speakers for participating in a very full day. You know several speakers arrived here late last night because they had other commitments. Getting up early and participating in this full day event is a lot, so we really want to give them a round of applause. I know I have learned an enormous amount today, and it has expanded my imagination and will inform the way I think and act in relation to the natural world. Again, thank you all, and we will see you next year.

Contributors

Dianne Bergant, Ph.D., C.S.A. (Catholic Theological Union)

Dianne Bergant, C.S.A. served as president of the Catholic Biblical Association of America in 2000–2001 and has been a member of the Chicago Catholic/Jewish Scholars Dialogue for more than twenty years. She has been the Old Testament book reviewer of *The Bible Today*, where she also was a member of the editorial board for twenty-five years — five of those as the magazine's general editor. From 2002 through 2005, she wrote the weekly column "The Word," for *America* magazine. She is on the editorial board of *Biblical Theology Bulletin* and *Chicago Studies*. Her many publications include *A Word for Every Season: Reflections on the Lectionary Readings Cycle C* (Paulist Press, 2009); *A Word for Every Season: Reflections on the Lectionary Readings Cycle B* (Paulist Press, 2008); *Preaching the New Lectionary, Year A* (Liturgical Press, 1999); *Preaching the New Lectionary, Year B* (Liturgical Press, 1999); *Preaching the New Lectionary, Year C* (Liturgical Press, 2000); *People of the Covenant: An Invitation to the Old Testament* (Sheed and Ward, 2001); and *Song of Songs: The Love Poetry of Scripture* (New City Press, 1998). She presently holds the chair of Distinguished Professor of Christian Culture at Providence College in Providence, Rhode Island, where she is working in the areas of biblical interpretation and biblical theology, particularly issues of peace, ecology, and feminism.

Daniel K. Finn, Ph.D. (St. John's University, Collegeville, Minnesota)

Daniel Finn is Professor of Moral Theology and William and Virginia Clemens Professor of Economics and the Liberal Arts at St. John's University in Collegeville, Minnesota. He is president of the Society of Christian Ethics and is a past-president of the Catholic

148

Theological Society of America and the Association for Social Economics. His most recent book is *The Moral Ecology of Markets: A Framework for Assessing Justice in Economic Life* (Cambridge University Press, 2006).

Richard W. Miller, Ph.D. (Creighton University)

Richard Miller is Assistant Professor of Systematic Theology and director of the M.A. in Theology at Creighton University. His scholarly interests are several: the problem of reconciling the Christian doctrine of providence with evil and human suffering, the notion of God as mystery, the implications of the doctrine of the Trinity for ontology, the thought of Karl Rahner and Thomas Aquinas as resources for contemporary theology, Catholicism and American public life, and climate change and social justice. He is a contributor to and editor of several volumes: *Women and the Shaping of Catholicism: Women through the Ages* (Ligouri, 2009); *We Hold These Truths: Catholicism and American Public Life* (Ligouri, 2008); *Prayer in the Catholic Tradition* (Ligouri, 2007); *Spirituality for the 21st Century: Experiencing God in the Catholic Tradition* (Ligouri, 2006); *Lay Ministry in the Catholic Church: Visioning Church Ministry through the Wisdom of the Past* (Ligouri, 2005). He has published in the *Heythrop Journal* and has articles forthcoming in the *Journal for Peace and Justice Studies, New Blackfriars,* and *Believing in Community: Ecumenical Reflections on the Church* (Peeters Press).

David J. O'Brien, Ph.D. (University of Dayton)

John O'Brien is Professor Emeritus of Catholic Studies at the College of the Holy Cross and University Professor of Faith and Culture at the University of Dayton. He has served as president of the American Catholic Historical Association. Among his six books is *Public Catholicism* (Orbis, 2nd ed., 1996) He speaks and writes widely on Catholics and politics.

John J. O'Keefe, Ph.D. (Creighton University)

John O'Keefe is Professor of Theology at Creighton University. He received his M.T.S. from Weston Jesuit School of Theology in 1987, and his M.A. and Ph.D. in Early Christian Studies from the Catholic University of America in 1990 and 1993. He has published widely on the history and theology of ancient Christianity, especially in the area of ancient interpretation of the Bible including together with R. R. Reno, *Sanctified Vision: An Introduction to Early Christian Interpretation of the Bible* (Johns Hopkins University Press, 2005). He is currently working on projects that explore Christian theologies of nature and the Christian contribution to the environmental movement. He joined the faculty of Creighton University in 1992. He served as chair of the Department of Theology for seven years and was recently named the next holder of the A. F. Jacobson Chair in Communication. He is married and has four children. John and his wife, Kathy, are members of Ignatian Associates, a lay association sharing in the mission and spirituality of the Society of Jesus.

Jame Schaefer, Ph.D. (Marquette University)

Jame Schaefer is Associate Professor of Systematic Theology and Ethics at Marquette University, where she specializes in the constructive relationship between theology and the natural sciences, directs the Interdisciplinary Minor in Environmental Ethics, and serves as Faculty Advisor of Students for an Environmentally Active Campus. Prior to her career in academia, Dr. Schaefer held leadership positions in local and regional environmental advocacy organizations and served in various capacities at the appointment of county, state, and national governments. She is the author of *Theological Foundations for Environmental Ethics: Reconstructing Patristic and Medieval Concepts* (Georgetown University Press, 2009).